Words of praise for Rick Winston a

"*Save Me a Seat!* is a chronicle of a lifetime love affair with cinema. Rick Winston carries his enthusiasm for the New York City independent theaters' fare of the '50s and '60s to the Green Mountains of Vermont, where it takes root in virgin cinematic soil. He describes the origins and growth of a community of film lovers far from the traditional centers of popular culture. Every page throbs with Winston's passion for movies. If you love movies, you will love this book."

–**Paul Hirsch,** Oscar-winning film editor and author of
A Long Time Ago in a Cutting Room Far, Far Away . . .

"Pop some corn, pour a drink and find a comfy chair. You'll want to settle in for this autobiography framed by the author's consuming love for film. *Save Me a Seat!* is part romp and part documentary, culled from Rick Winston's earliest moments as a fanboy in the 1950s to his years as an encyclopedic cinema owner and teacher decades later. Serious cinephiles and casual moviegoers alike will enjoy the show."

–**Pamela Polston,** co-founder and art editor of *Seven Days*

"This memoir by one of the early heroes of film culture brings back the adventure of moviegoing in the glorious heyday of that phenomenon. Establishing a beach-head in Vermont, Rick has done it all as teacher, programmer, and finally running a theater and opening a video store. The bumps and joys of his journey, the portraits of the films and people he encounters along the way, make for a buoyant read. This is an irresistible feast for serious moviegoers."

–**Molly Haskell,** film critic and author of *Steven Spielberg: A Life in Films.*

"Author and film scholar Rick Winston tells us the genesis story of Vermont's landmark Savoy Theater, which for decades has satisfied the cinematic hunger of Vermonters. But beyond starting the Lightning Ridge Film Society in 1973 that evolved into the Savoy, for so many of us Rick was the scholar and educator about a broader film culture. This outstanding memoir and history encompasses both the origins of the Savoy and the naissance of a film culture in Vermont that understood film both as art and entertainment."

–**Bill Schubart,** author of *Lila & Theron*

"Winston's book is an immensely engaging personal history that any passionate filmgoer will instantly relate to. By reliving his lifelong love of movies, he also allows us to relive our own."

–**Peter Rainer,** Pulitzer Prize finalist in criticism, author of
*Rainer on Film: Thirty Years of Film Writing in a Turbulent and
Transformative Era*

"As huge film lovers, whose independent distribution company we started from scratch 34 years ago, we identified mightily with both Rick Winston's great satisfaction as well as the tribulations he experienced in starting his wonderful Savoy Theater. And as tremendous fans of Rick we couldn't be happier that he put this fascinating account down on paper for others to read and be inspired by. It's a vivid personal history of a world that is relevant to everyone who loves movies, from audiences of a 'certain age' to twenty-somethings who have just discovered the marvelous world of repertory and specialized cinema."

–**Nancy Gerstman** and **Emily Russo,** Zeitgeist Films

"Anyone who opens an art or repertory cinema, especially one in a small town, should have their head examined. But we should all be grateful to dreamers like Rick Winston, who've managed to turn their young passions into, not just careers, but into cultural touchstones that enrich everyone. Add Rick's charming book to the rarefied few that explain how."

–**Bruce Goldstein,** founder of Rialto Pictures and
repertory artistic director of New York's Film Forum

"Rick Winston's passion for movies led to a lifetime devoted to advocacy—and to bringing contemporary and classic films to new audiences. He writes with verve and joy about great movies (*Children of Paradise, Sullivan's Travels*) as well as can't-miss films that are less well known, such as the British anthology picture *Dead of Night*. What Rick has written is, in effect, a charming autobiography in the form of a chronicle of a love affair with an art form."

–**David Lehman,** author of *The Mysterious Romance of Murder:
Crime, Detection, and the Spirit of Noir*

"Graham Greene said he'd 'like to write the biography of an inimitable movie house.' Rick Winston has done just that! In this splendid memoir, he exhibits the most generous writing ethic: sustaining an intimate tone while at the same time providing a behind-the-scenes education. Also, with just his second book, Rick has become an indispensable historian of Vermont, who can bring the political and emotional dimensions of a given decade to us with vivid immediacy. Late last night, reading certain passages aloud as if to ghosts, it felt as if decades of Savoy evenings knocked on our farmhouse door, and we had a joyful reunion."

–**Howard Norman,** author of *Come to the Window*

Save Me A Seat!

2002 Green Mountain Film Festival cover art by Anne Davis.

Save Me Me
A Seat!

A Life With Movies

Rick Winston

Montpelier, Vermont

Save Me A Seat! A Life With Movies

Rick Winston

Release Date: August 29, 2023

First Printing: 2023

Copyright: 2022

Published by Rootstock Publishing
32 Main Street #165, Montpelier, VT 05602

info@rootstockpublishing.com

Paperback Print ISBN: 978-1-57869-128-9

Library of Congress Control Number: 2022920874

eBook ISBN: 978-1-57869-130-2

Hardcover ISBN: 978-1-57869-129-6

Cover and Book Design: Mason Singer, Laughing Bear Associates

Front cover photo: © Emma Norman

Back Cover photo: © Jeb Wallace-Brodeur

Printed in the USA

For permissions or to schedule an author interview,
contact the author at vtcrostic@gmail.com.

For Andrea,
partner in life
and movies

TABLE OF CONTENTS

2004 Green Mountain Film Festival cover art by Ed Koren.

INTRODUCTION

Barry Snyder
former chair of cinema studies and
film production at Burlington College

Rick Winston's genial and companionable memoir is the chronicle of a lifelong love affair with movies. Movies, the pleasure of movies, the ways in which movies bring people and communities together and change lives, movies in general and movies in particular, fill the book. The telling has the pleasant feel of a conversation with a very knowledgeable friend about films, about experiences seeing films, about connections to other moviegoers and to the world at large by way of film, and about people, including renowned critics and filmmakers, met along the way. The taste is maple syrup on popcorn, the flavoring courtesy of Winston's fateful decision, as a still young man and erstwhile urbanite, to settle in a farmhouse in rural Vermont, a move that presaged the most unlikely and unique part of his story: his founding of the Green Mountain State's first and only genuine "art house" movie theater, the Savoy.

For cinephiles, the general arc of his story up to that point will be familiar: his early exposure to the idea of something special about movies (Winston credits his movie-loving dad), his discovery of classic American films on TV, and his growing awareness of the larger world of films through books on the history of cinema. A bit further down the road, his knowledge and appreciation of films would expand through exposure to the curated offerings, including foreign films, of legendary art house theaters like the Thalia, the Bleecker Street Cinema, and the New Yorker in New York City and, during what he describes as a turbulent year at the University of California, the Telegraph Repertory Cinema in Berkeley.

Where Winston's particular case of cinephilia takes a more singular turn follows his move to Vermont, lured, like so many others of similar age, by the back-to-the-land enthusiasm that abounded in the 1960s. Like other "urban refugees," Winston was disappointed by the scarcity of cultural amenities in rural Vermont, and particularly the absence of the kinds and quantities of films he had become used to seeing—needed to see—as a condition of his affliction. The serendipitous solution—to start his own film society, leading to the creation of a theater in a building and space that coincidentally turned out to have housed one in the nickelodeon era—was the turning point of his professional life.

Winston's personable, anecdotal style, in recollecting the details of that story, suggests the kind of conversations one might have had chatting with him over the counter next to the popcorn machine at the Savoy, or getting advice about a movie rental from his wife, Andrea Serota, at the checkout counter of Downstairs Video, the "cultural speakeasy" the couple established in the basement of the theater. The familiar and homey feeling accords with what turned out to be, along with its other charms, a genuine "mom and pop" operation. Even those who do not know Rick and Andrea will come away from the book having gained detailed knowledge of what running a movie theater, a rental store, and a ten-day film festival looks like on an up-close-and-personal, day-to-day basis. For anyone who knows the movies only from the comfortable viewpoint of a seat in the theater, the complexities and challenges of what goes on behind the scenes to get a movie in front of viewers will surely enlighten.

None of which is to suggest a story lacking in larger significance, even if the author himself is reluctant to locate it there. Winston's personal story is part of a much larger story of momentous cultural changes and generational shifts that followed in the wake of World War II, including major structural changes in the film industry itself, brought about by a government antitrust lawsuit forcing studios to divest of their theaters. This resulted in the collapse of the monopolistic system of production, distribution, and exhibition that characterized the studio system in its prime.

Among the most iconic of the art house theaters that arose in the aftermath of the so-called Paramount Decision were the very ones Winston attended as a young man, where he developed his taste for, and education about, the richnesses of cinema beyond what he could find in theaters forced to follow the dictates of the studios that owned them. Winston's story subsequently reveals the cause-and-effect linkage between the rise of art house theaters in the 1950s, the cultivation of a taste for varieties of cinema (foreign films, independent films, documentaries) beyond the mainstream, and the formation of a renewed "film culture" that produced both cinephiles like Winston and filmmakers whose artistic ambitiousness revitalized and transformed cinema.

To appreciate what those changes meant for anyone interested in movies, one has to recall how hard it was, in the days before DVDs or movie channels or streaming platforms or VOD (video on demand), to see a film again after its initial theatrical run or, indeed, a film that never made it to a theater near you at all. In the 1970s, when Winston's Lightning Ridge Film Society screened programs in Montpelier's Pavilion Auditorium (his first effort to curate programs of films for others), it would have been virtually impossible, outside of a university class or art house repertory screening, for the general public to view films like Fritz Lang's *The Testament of Dr. Mabuse* (1933), Preston Sturges's *Sullivan's Travels* (1941), or Stanley Kubrick's *The Killing* (1956), to cite just three examples from the Film Society's inaugural 1973 program. As one of Lightning Ridge's then youthful patrons testifies, exposure to a film as artistically provocative as Spanish filmmaker Luis Buñuel's surreal 1962 masterpiece *The Exterminating Angel* constituted a literally unforgettable experience of the kind that haunts one forever. But these were experiences one could not get by going down the street to rent a movie, and could enjoy only rarely by sitting with an audience to watch a projected film in a theater.

Even more culturally impactful than Winston's Film Society was the founding of the Savoy in 1981. If Montpelier was the political capital of Vermont, the college-rich city of Burlington, with close to five times the population of Montpelier's eight thousand, was ostensibly the state's cultural capital. Despite that, Burlington in the 1980s had no theater given to screening foreign films, small independent and regional films, and documentaries of the sort that became the main-stays of the Savoy, apart from the (short-lived, in terms of its bona fides as an art house) Nickelodeon. (The fate of the Nickelodeon, soon sold to a larger theater chain and thereby gaining access to a "circuit" of film distribution, hints at the extraordinary challenges faced by truly independent theaters like the Savoy.) During the next two decades, the Savoy would come to be regarded as the secular version of a holy place among Vermont cinéastes; traveling down or up to Montpelier to catch a film one wouldn't be able to see otherwise became a kind of pilgrimage.

For people who lived near Montpelier, the Savoy meant something more. Although the Savoy fits most comfortably in the category of the art house theater, it was also the kind of theater that, in the studio era, distributors would have referred to as a "nabe," which is to say, a theater strongly identified with the neighborhood in which it was located. If the Savoy was not quite the exaggerated fantasy of a remembered communal center depicted in Italian director Giuseppe Tornatore's *Cinema Paradiso* (1988), it was nevertheless intertwined with the people and life of Montpelier well beyond the norm, in ways that Winston's memoir details. For all its physical smallness, there was something large about its personality and its entanglement with the life of the community that is in stark contrast to the anonymous subur-ban multiplexes whose rise and dominance began during this same period. By comparison to these anodyne theaters, the Savoy recalled, painfully, all that was being lost.

One additional dimension of the impact of Winston's intervention in Vermont's cultural scene deserves further comment. A symbiotic relationship can be traced between the education to be gained from cultural expressions like movies (especially movies, in their ability to speak across barriers in a language accessible to all) and the social, political, and historical consciousness of the people exposed to them. In this case, the Savoy, and even more so the annual Green Mountain

Film Festival that Winston, with the help of others, established in 1999, using the Savoy as its primary venue, made an explicit contribution to the social and political fermentation that characterized this period of Vermont's history.

Winston himself had been brought up to be attuned to the social and political dimensions of the movies he watched in his youth, courtesy of parents who were themselves victims of the notorious Red Scare, and that particular strand of his sensibility is evident throughout his career as a film programmer. Without doubt, by screening fiction and nonfiction films rich in sociological, historical, and political content, films about world events, films that gave people visions of life in distant places beyond the distorting view of government propaganda or the gentler but no less pernicious obfuscations of entertainment films, the Savoy and the Green Mountain Film Festival added to the cultural soup that fed the nascent political consciousness and socially progressive activism with which the state would soon become identified. It was part of a generational shift in the identity of Vermont following an influx of young people that included Winston himself, and of which Winston's fellow New York transplant Bernie Sanders is the exemplar.

But one need not have been of that time or have partaken of its zeitgeist to enjoy this memoir. On the contrary, Winston's taste in movies, and subsequently his orientation in presenting films to the public as programmer, educator, and now as author, is inclusive, multigenerational, and never didactic. Winston incites passion by sharing the details of his own, not by talking abstractly about cinema. Individual movies and individual movie experiences, highlighted and discussed in the text and "trailers," are the girders upon which the book, like his life, is built. It's as much an invitation to join him at the movies as it is a memoir. I'm certain you'll have a good time.

–Barry Snyder, 2022

2003 Green Mountain Film Festival cover art by Ed Epstein.

PART 1

A FILM EDUCATION
1947-1969

CHAPTER 1

AWAKENINGS

"Time to get up ... Erich von Stroheim died."
Possibly other ten-year-old boys would wake up to the news that Mickey Mantle had hit a game-winning homer, but on May 13, 1957, this is how my father, Leon, chose to start my day.

When I was growing up in Yonkers, New York, Leon was the one who woke my younger brother Jon and me. My mother, Julia, had already left for the day, going into Manhattan to teach at the High School of Music and Art. Leon owned an art-supplies store in a nearby shopping center and had a much more leisurely morning, listening to the classical music station WQXR and then making sure we were off to school.

Leon was a passionate film buff who passed that love on to me. I look back at that morbid news bulletin as an emblematic moment, in which he recognized the budding film fan in me. I was still quite a few years away from seeing von Stroheim's two best-known roles, in

Erich von Stroheim
as drawn by John Held, Jr.

La Grande Illusion and *Sunset Boulevard,* but I must have already known who the Viennese director and actor was. Perhaps it was from films shown on TV's *The Early Show* or *Million Dollar Movie*. Perhaps it was from magazine caricatures of the bald, monocled von Stroheim, with his air of menace, who was known during his career as "The Man You Loved to Hate." Perhaps it was from images in the *Life* magazine repository in our garage going back to the late 1930s, my own private library on days home from school.

Although Leon's training was in architecture and art history, he was the kind of film lover who remembered every film he ever saw, plus where and when he saw it. If such qualities are, in some way, genetic, I certainly inherited them. He would enthusiastically recall films he had seen, especially if they had a social message, such as the 1930s crime dramas *They Gave Him a Gun, Fury,* and *They Won't Forget.* I had only one occasion to silently curse him for his memory display. That was when I was finally old enough to see Georges Clouzot's *Diabolique* in revival and unfortunately still remembered the film's twist ending as related by Leon years before. I won't give it away here.

Leon didn't always own an art-supplies store. He had been an art teacher for many years, at Taft High School in the Bronx, but in the early 1950s he became a victim of the "Red Scare," specifically the purge of left-leaning members of the New York City Teachers' Union. One of his star students in the 1940s, Harvey Matusow, had by 1953 become a paid informer for the House Un-American Activities Committee. Matusow named my father at a Washington, D.C., hearing on "Communist Influence in Education." (At a hearing that same day on "Communist Influence in Entertainment," Matusow also named folksingers Woody Guthrie, Brownie McGhee, Pete Seeger, and Tom Paley, so Leon was in good company.)

Leon resigned before an inevitable firing, but my mother Julia, also in danger of losing her job, was able to continue teaching through an accident of timing. Her "invitation" to appear before a New York City Board of Education investigating committee came three years after Leon's, in 1956. Before then, many of my parents' colleagues had been fired as a result of the 1949 "Feinberg Law," which stated that any city employee who did not cooperate with an investigation (i.e., inform on others) would be dismissed. But by 1956, a suit challenging that law was in process; Julia could not be fired for refusing to give names while the appeal—ultimately successful—was pending. She continued teaching until her retirement in 1974.

Leon at Taft High School in the Bronx.

No wonder that my parents, with their progressive backgrounds, were so excited to see, and introduce me to, any film that had some political or social significance, whether *The Defiant Ones, The Diary of Anne Frank, Judgment at Nuremberg,* or a little-known Bette Davis film from 1956, *Storm Center,* in which she played a librarian accused of leftist leanings. Antiwar films, like *Ballad of a Soldier,* also piqued their interest. They were especially eager to take me to see Stanley Kubrick's *Paths of Glory,* a powerful film set in the French trenches during World War I.

Many critics took notice of Kubrick's talent for the first time with this film, made in 1957 when he was barely thirty years old, but Leon had an inside scoop: Kubrick had been a student at Taft High School, in the class of 1946. Although Kubrick did not take a class with him, Leon, like most other faculty members, was familiar with this extraordinary, yet problematic student. As Leon related the story, Stanley's teachers exclaimed in frustration, "He's such a brilliant kid, but cuts school to hang out in Times Square with his camera. What's going to become of him?"

There were several nearby theaters where I saw some of my earliest films. The Central (on Central Avenue, naturally) was within walking distance of home, and just a little farther away were the Kent and the

KRUH, PHYLLIS   Library Aide, War Bonds and Stamps Salesman.   Inside the school she's quiet as a mouse; but outside—I wonder!

KRULIK, HERBERT A.   Service Aide to Dr. Mandel, Locker Room Aide.   Here is a boy who looks as if he is ready to do something.   When will he do it?

KUBRICK, STANLEY   Taft Review, School Band.   When he was on the TAFT REVIEW, you always found him in a stew.

Everyone at Taft knew the underachieving Stanley Kubrick.

Kimball. Sometimes my grandmother, Lizzie, would take me to the Central; her favorites were musicals and romances. Other times, it was my older brother, Winnie, whose tastes ran to physical comedy, horror, and science fiction.

Poor Winnie. On three occasions, he had to take me home in tears. Once was during a Laurel and Hardy short in which Oliver is in traction with a broken leg, and somehow the doctor winds up dangling from a ninth-floor window. (Much later, when I was ordering VHS tapes for the Savoy Theater's video store, I identified it as *County Hospital.*)

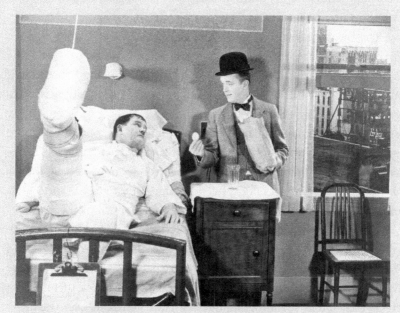

Too much for me: Stan and Ollie in *County Hospital*.

All I remember from the second film, a Three Stooges short, was violence.[1] And the third was a film set in the Caribbean. At age seven, my introduction to the practice of voodoo, as represented in that film anyway, was more than I could tolerate. I do remember making it through the giant-ants-invade-earth spectacle *Them!* and the sci-fi thriller *Gog*.

Beyond the main drag in our Yonkers neighborhood, another world beckoned. Though we now lived in the suburbs, my parents, Bronx dwellers until 1948, were true cosmopolitans. This meant an interest not only in classical music and museums, but in foreign films as well. I could picture them in the late 1930s, going to see *Alexander Nevsky* (Sergei

---

[1]Years later, I discovered that Moe was born Moses Horwitz and that the Horwitz family had emigrated to the United States from Vilna, Lithuania. Not just any old city in the old country, but the very seat of Jewish scholarship, home to the original YIVO Center for Jewish Research. The juxtaposition of the Stooges' antics with the Vilna fountain of knowledge is one of many bizarre instances of the ingredients that make up the brew that is American popular culture.

Eisenstein's Soviet epic) and *The Baker's Wife* (Marcel Pagnol's French classic) as a part of their cultural life.

The theater nearest Yonkers that showcased foreign films was the Pix in White Plains, and it was there, also when I was seven, that I saw my first foreign film, Jacques Tati's *M. Hulot's Holiday*. It had few if any subtitles, but its picture of a seaside resort where vacationers were desperate to enjoy themselves was quite accessible. I was completely taken with Tati's well-meaning but bumbling Hulot, whose efforts to ingratiate himself with his companions invariably led to disaster. Tati, a former music hall performer and an extraordinary mime, brought back M. Hulot on several occasions; his next film, *Mon Oncle,* from 1958, is another of his equally delightful films that my parents took me to see.

I'm not sure that Leon and Julia had a strictly pedagogical purpose in mind when they took me to see films like *Mon Oncle* or *Ballad of a Soldier,* but the message I took away was clear: there are other worlds and peoples beyond our own limited horizon, and we can learn from them. That might seem like an obvious statement, but over the years I came to understand that Americans are encouraged to have minimal curiosity or imagination about other places on earth.

I'm reminded of a story that my friend Ray Neinstein told, about his first year teaching freshman English at SUNY Buffalo. Ray was on his way to class one day when he noticed a sign on the auditorium door announcing a showing that afternoon of François Truffaut's *Shoot the Piano Player.* Ray posted a sign on his own classroom door directing students to go see the film and write three pages on it. He only realized later that for some it was their first experience with a foreign film and subtitles. One student complained in the paper, "I don't see why they had to go all the way to France and find people who spoke French—why didn't they just make the movie here?"

▣ TRAILER:
REAR WINDOW

Whenever I give a presentation of Alfred Hitchcock films or, in particular, when I teach *Rear Window*, I always take a moment to thank my parents. Whatever possessed them to assume that *Rear Window*, still one of the most suspenseful films ever made, was appropriate for a seven-year-old? It was a Thanksgiving weekend outing to the Parkway, a classy Art Deco theater in nearby Mount Vernon, and there I had one of my formative film experiences.

The Parkway Theater in Mount Vernon, N.Y.

In this movie, based on the Cornell Woolrich short story "It Had to Be Murder," James Stewart is wheelchair-bound with a broken leg and out of boredom takes to spying on his neighbors. He comes to suspect that one of them is a killer, engages in flirtatious double-entendre with the glamorous Grace Kelly, and then has his life threatened by the villain (played by a pre–Perry Mason Raymond Burr). Although I was too young to appreciate the way Hitchcock (and his ace screenwriter, John Michael Hayes) used sly humor to provide an entrée into the story, I was part of the rapt audience Hitchcock had in mind as he used all his skills to make us gradually identify with Stewart's predicament. It's said that at the premiere, Hitchcock was sitting with Gloria Stewart, James Stewart's wife. Grabbing the director's arm at a certain crucial point, she frantically whispered, "Do something!!"

Another child might have hidden under the seat, or cried to go home, or had nightmares for a week. But I was enthralled and at some level aware of the craft that went into the creation of a spellbinding atmosphere. I couldn't have expressed the feeling then, but my visceral reaction was an introduction to the thesis that not all movies are created equal. Maybe I even said to my parents, "Hitchcock? Is that the name?"

James Stewart, Grace Kelly, and Alfred Hitchcock on the set of *Rear Window*.

I thought of this auspicious night at the movies many years later, when I was invited by my friend Barry Snyder, then head of Burlington College's film department, to become an adjunct instructor there. When we discussed which course I would teach, he said, "Well, there hasn't been a Hitchcock class in a while . . . " I quickly discovered why Hitchcock is so beloved not just by audiences, but by film instructors: in a career that spanned several important eras in film history, he used motifs (or, as some say, obsessions) that could be followed from *The Lodger* in 1925 straight through to his final film, in 1976, *Family Plot*.

My students at Burlington had all grown up with computer-generated special effects and had been watching action-packed crowd-pleasers for many years. Nevertheless, they became spellbound as the claustrophobic, slow-drip suspense of *Rear Window* took hold. They savored the display of Hitchcock's favorite motifs and themes: the ordinary person caught up in an extraordinary event, an icy-cool blonde as the romantic interest, and a fascination with the very act of watching. I couldn't have been more pleased to observe how this class discovered for themselves the thrill I experienced as an awestruck seven-year-old.

The film remains one of my favorites—to watch, to show, and to teach—almost seventy years later.

◫ TRAILER:
THE HORSE'S MOUTH

Thanks to our family outings to the Pix, I became an Alec Guinness admirer at an early age. I especially loved his idealistic inventor in *The Man in the White Suit* and his mild-mannered bank clerk who masterminds a heist in *The Lavender Hill Mob*, both comedies from London's famed Ealing Studios. I would rewatch these on television whenever they appeared, along with another Ealing comedy, *Kind Hearts and Coronets*, in which he played eight roles. My parents may have noted my fondness for Guinness as they planned a festive New Year's Day outing in 1958. We went to Manhattan's chic Paris Theater to see Guinness' new film, *The Horse's Mouth*.

The Horse's Mouth: Alec Guinness as a *monstre sacré.*

Here was a very different Guinness performance. He played Gulley Jimson, a visionary William Blake–quoting artist who cannot see a blank wall without imagining a heroic mural. This Guinness was neither the bright young man nor the timid bank clerk. He was a scruffy and conniving scamp, with a gruff voice and little patience for anyone who couldn't understand his art. Whether making prank phone calls, bossing his worshipful young assistant, or quoting William Blake, Guinness channeled the colorful and volatile Jimson.

He set a new standard for acting in my growing awareness of that mysterious craft that so resembles alchemy.

In those days, I was so impatient for a film to begin that I didn't pay much attention to opening credits (and there were opening credits in those days). I noticed that Alec Guinness was the star but did not register that the screenplay was his as well. He had adapted Joyce Cary's 1944 novel of the same name. Guinness first read the novel while serving on a Royal Navy ship during World War II. Though he was at first put off by Cary's stream of consciousness style, he later read it again at his wife Merula's suggestion. He saw the filmic possibilities, and his enthusiasm led producer John Bryan and director Ronald Neame to sign on to this long-gestating labor of love.

The Horse's Mouth film also made me a lifelong enthusiast for the music of Sergei Prokofiev. Though it seems likely that, like many ten-year-olds, I had heard "Peter and the Wolf," it was the "Lieutenant Kije Suite," used in Guinness' film, that captured my imagination.

Prokofiev had written this music for a 1931 Russian film. The idea of using this score, with each of its five sections appropriate to a different mood of the film, came from Joyce Cary himself. Cary's son Tristram, a composer for film and television, had scored Guinness' 1956 film *The Ladykillers*. One of Tristram Cary's final conversations with his father, who died in 1957, touched on the film that was now in production and what music might be appropriate. The film's director, Ronald Neame, recalled in his memoir, *Straight From the Horse's Mouth*, that Joyce Cary suggested something "jaunty and cocky like 'Lieutenant Kije.'" Though Tristram Cary was not ultimately the one adapting Prokofiev's score (that is credited to Kenneth Jones), the connection was made.

There was a lot to entertain a ten-year-old in the film: colorful characters, antic behavior, and chase sequences set to Prokofiev. But on revisiting the film as an adult, I discovered its darker side. The film portrayed—through the genius of Guinness—the artist as an iconoclast condemned by his vision to be an outsider in polite society. The film is also a disturbing study of a *monstre sacré*, that useful French phrase: a narcissist so dedicated to his art that he is oblivious to the consequences of his behavior. The ones who suffer are those who care for him the most.

CHAPTER 2

THANK YOU,
MILLION DOLLAR MOVIE

A fter many years of living in Vermont, I had one of those dreams that put me back in college (in my case, Columbia University) with one more semester to go. Ever the optimist, I reasoned in my dream, "Well, at least I'll have access to all those great TV stations." My unconscious seemed to be in touch with the television of my youth, when several local stations (WNEW, WPIX, WNVA, and WOR) had schedules to fill and often plugged the gaps with old films. Back then, I didn't have to go to revival houses in Manhattan to experience the richness of Hollywood film. Whether they were classics or not, they were right there in my Yonkers bedroom.

After my initial traumatic Laurel and Hardy experience at the Central Theater, I came to appreciate and enjoy their humor—and that of the Marx Brothers—on Saturday afternoons. I also saw countless low-budget westerns from Republic Studios, thanks to Channel 13, in the years before its emergence as New York's public television station WNET. Roy Rogers and Gene Autry never appealed to me; my tastes ran to Hopalong Cassidy and Johnny Mack Brown. I especially admired obscure stars like Sunset Carson (whose snazzy black shirt I coveted) and Robert Livingston, who played a character called Stoney Brooke in a series of films featuring "The Three Mesquiteers."

It's true—this future pacifist grew up on a steady diet of shoot-'em-up westerns (like Samuel Fuller's *I Shot Jesse James*) and war films (like

Above left: I loved Sunset Carson's black shirt. Right: "It was just a little walk/ In that warm Italian sun . . ."

Fuller's *The Steel Helmet*). *A Walk in the Sun*, set during World War II's Italian campaign and directed by Lewis Milestone, was another favorite. Some in the excellent cast became my favorite actors: Dana Andrews, Richard Conte, Lloyd Bridges, John Ireland, and Sterling Holloway. That film had a seal of approval from my parents, as the memorable songs in it were written by progressives Earl Robinson and Millard Lampell.

Sometimes I fixated on odd films, watching them each time they were aired. One was *The Villain Still Pursued Her*, a 1940 parody of old-fashioned stage melodramas. It was my first sighting of Buster Keaton, who was then at a low point in his career, an alcoholic lucky to get any parts. Years later, when I saw his earlier films, his genius and physical grace astounded me. I could hardly reconcile the angelic (and silent) young man I was seeing then with the beaten-down and raspy-voiced actor I had watched in that 1940 film.

Another of my favorites was a low-budget action thriller made in 1950, *Western Pacific Agent*. This film now qualifies as a "forgotten noir," according to one DVD company publicist. Just as I appreciated the B-list western leads, I much preferred lower-echelon actors such as Robert Lowery, who played the hero of that film, to the bigger Hollywood names. *Western Pacific Agent* also featured two actors who became victims of the Hollywood blacklist, just taking hold in Hollywood: Mickey Knox, who had to emigrate to Europe in order to find work,

Morris Carnovsky and Mickey Knox in *Western Pacific Agent*.

and Morris Carnovsky, a founding member of New York's famed Group Theater, who returned to the stage after he became unemployable in Hollywood.

Another blacklist casualty, Carl Foreman, was responsible for an obscure comedy that made my own cult-film list at the time: *So This Is New York*. The 1948 film was based on a Ring Lardner short story and starred Henry Morgan, then a major radio personality. It had a strain of madcap humor that made me laugh uproariously at age ten—but not so much now. While watching it again a few years ago, I couldn't take the strained humor longer than the half-hour mark.

But like so many other nascent film buffs growing up in the New York City area, I can't talk about films on television without fondly recalling the program *Million Dollar Movie*. This series began in New York City, on a local station, WOR-TV, Channel 9, in 1955. It ran for more than a decade, featuring top-tier American movies. Each feature would run for an entire week, airing twice nightly and, if I recall correctly, once again on Saturday and Sunday.[2] This was the show that Martin Scorsese credited with much of his film education; in his opinion, we young viewers became film critics without even knowing it.

I watched *King Kong* every night that week.

As WOR was a subsidiary of RKO General Tire, many of those films were free to the station. Those RKO films included *King Kong, Gunga Din, Citizen Kane,* and the Fred Astaire-Ginger Rogers RKO musicals.

---

[2]Many people who grew up in the New York City area have *Million Dollar Movie* stories. My favorite is from a friend, Jacob Stone, who was ten years old the night *King Kong* premiered. It happened to be the same night as a coed party—a first!—that his sister was hosting. Unfortunately, all the boys at the party decamped to Jacob's room to watch the film. "My sister's eighty-one years old now," says Jacob, "and I don't think she's ever forgiven me."

Sometimes the films were edited to fit the ninety-minute slot, including commercials. But even if the films were chopped up, any night of the week I could watch Fay Wray fighting off King Kong or the faithful water carrier played by Sam Jaffe saving the British army.

Like Scorsese, actor John Turturro credited the show with an outsized influence on his life. He has said it was watching *Million Dollar Movie*—and especially Burt Lancaster films—as a kid in Queens that made him want to become an actor. He even included an homage in *Mac,* his first film as a director, playing a fictionalized version of his own father. In one scene, Turturro's Mac, exhausted from construction work, dozes on the couch as his family watches the drama *From Here to Eternity* on television (presumably *Million Dollar Movie*). He awakens to exclaim, "Nobody fucks with Burt Lancaster!"

Nancy Guild and George Montgomery: *The Brasher Doubloon.*

Film critic Peter Rainer also credits *Million Dollar Movie* with sparking his interest in films: "I am convinced that the show set an entire crop of kids on the road to a critic's connoisseurship," he wrote in *Rainer on Film.* "By week's end, you could memorize how a movie was put together, whether it was *The Hunchback of Notre Dame* with Charles Laughton or *The Body Snatcher* with Boris Karloff."

One film I remember intently watching night after night was a murder mystery called *The Brasher Doubloon.* And one image—of the victim being pushed from a high window—held a particular fascination for me. Years later, I discovered that this film was an adaptation of Raymond Chandler's novel *The High Window*, with Robert Montgomery as Chandler's dogged detective, Philip Marlowe. I was pleased to learn that in the opinion of some critics, the film has been unjustly neglected. Dave Kehr, who is among my favorite film critics, put it this way in his *Chicago Reader* column: "What keeps the last third afloat owes less to Chandler . . . than to the sense of brooding Gothic melodrama in which [director John] Brahm specialized." Perhaps I was already developing an eye for stark contrasts and intense atmosphere.[3]

Whether through westerns, gangster films, or comedies, I was constantly absorbing distinctive images from those films of the 1930s and '40s. The movies gave me an idea of American life in the years before my birth—at least how it was presented by Hollywood, and in black and white.

Like so many other movie fans, I loved the magnetic stars—Edward G. Robinson, Katharine Hepburn, James Cagney, and Humphrey Bogart. But I also became an aficionado, long before I knew that word, of that immense army of character actors that populated those old films: Donald Meek, Helen Broderick, Jane Darwell, and Billy Gilbert, to name just a few.

Thanks largely to *Million Dollar Movie,* I never developed that malady so common to younger people of any generation: a reflexive disdain for any cultural artifact of a previous time.

---

[3]Our family didn't get our first color television until the mid-1960s.

TRAILER: CITIZEN KANE

One day Leon alerted me to an upcoming *Million Dollar Movie:* "I think you'll like this one, it's called *Citizen Kane.*" He then gave me some background on Orson Welles, who both directed and starred in the film. Welles had been a twenty-year-old wunderkind who took the world of stage and radio by storm in the late 1930s. My parents attended some of Welles' Mercury Theater productions in New York City and were regular listeners to his weekly CBS radio show. It was one of these shows, broadcast on Halloween, 1938, that gave Welles national notoriety: his adaptation of H.G. Wells' *War of the Worlds* convinced many terrified listeners that Martians had actually landed in New Jersey.

There are a few things I remember Leon telling me about the film. The first was that Welles, who was twenty-five at the time, played Kane first as a young man, then as a powerful man in his fifties, and then as a wreck of a man in extreme old age. The second was that the film had made-up newsreel footage that looked like the real thing.

There was another dimension

Citizen Kane: "What can you say about a man's life?"

to my father's passion about the film. It was, he explained, a thinly disguised portrait of the publisher William Randolph Hearst. Both of my mild-mannered parents displayed a visceral animosity when the subject of Hearst was raised. At any mention of the *New York Journal-American*, they would sneer, "What do you expect from a Hearst newspaper?"

Their vitriol had a personal component, as I would learn when I was finally old enough to hear about their experiences during the Red Scare.

Years before Senator Joseph McCarthy entered the political stage in 1950, Hearst was a chief promulgator of the anti-communist hysteria that engulfed the New York City Teachers' Union and cost my father his job. Historian Ellen Schrecker wrote in *Many Are the Crimes*, her history of the McCarthy Era, "Since the mid-1930s, the conservative press lord created a formidable network of professional red-baiters who brought the communists-as-subversives narrative into the political mainstream during the early Cold War."

As my knowledge of film history grew, I learned more about Hearst and the behind-the-scenes story of the *Citizen Kane* production. It was every bit as dramatic as the finished product. Welles' co-screenwriter Herman Mankiewicz had been a frequent visitor at Hearst's San Simeon castle and added atmospheric tidbits for Kane's own "Xanadu" pleasure palace. Hearst attempted to scuttle the film before it was released, offering RKO Pictures a grand sum to destroy the print. Film history would never have been the same had RKO taken his offer. After its release in December 1941, the film was never advertised in any Hearst newspapers.

It's always dangerous to build up a film too much, but in this case, Leon was right. I watched at least a part of it every night. By the end of the week, I knew it quite well, loving Welles' bravura touches. *Citizen Kane* didn't look like any other film from that era that I had watched on television. I was captivated by its montages that captured the passage of time, the way one scene gave way seamlessly to another, the striking use of light and shadow, and the use of sound to convey a sense of cavernous space. I was also fascinated by the progression of Charles Foster Kane from idealistic journalist to power-mad manipulator, with dire consequences for the people closest to him.

With repeated viewings over the years, I came to understand that *Citizen Kane* was an experimental masterpiece, as Welles and his collaborators (like cinematographer Gregg Toland, editor Robert Wise, and art director Perry Ferguson) broke new ground. There is no better teaching tool for introducing students to the many aspects of filmmaking. When I introduce it to young students, I stress that there are several ways to approach the film: just for starters, it's a mystery, a technical marvel, a character study, and a slice of turn-of-the-century American history. There is still always something new to notice in this monumental work of art.

CHAPTER 3

BUCK'S ROCK: MY SUMMER PLACE

In addition to the formative hours I spent watching *Million Dollar Movie,* I experienced an even greater influence each summer. I saw no more television in July and August, for my parents were counselors at an extraordinary summer camp, Buck's Rock, in New Milford, Connecticut.

Sometime during the school year of 1949–50, my mother's teaching colleague Harold "Hal" Loren suggested that she and Leon look into working at the camp where Hal had been a counselor the previous summer. According to Hal, it was a very creative, exciting place with forward-thinking educators at the helm. Besides, couldn't they use some money during the summer, while providing a country environment for their kids?

This was a fateful decision, for outside of my family's home, there was no place more significant in shaping the person I became. Other former campers have offered many testimonials to the camp's life-changing effect, but my experience was different from those who attended only in their teenage years. I was at Buck's Rock every summer (save one) from 1950, when I was three, to 1963. It was my childhood playground, my private school, my art colony, and my model of a creative community. It helped spark my interest in films, theater, music, and social justice, and it taught me valuable lessons about friendship. I observed—and sometimes took part in—a nonconformist ethos that flourished each summer. Years later, one counselor from that era looked back and wrote, "Anyone who was at Buck's Rock in the 1950s was well-prepared for the 1960s."

My mother, Julia, in the "Jewelry Shop."

The educators who had founded Buck's Rock were a Viennese couple, Ernst and Ilse Bulova, who had studied and worked in Germany in the 1930s, then fled first to England and then to the United States. They founded the camp in 1942 as part of the war effort, giving children from New York a chance to help rural farmers with "victory gardens." The Bulovas were influenced by the teachings of the educator Maria Montessori, who believed that work could be both play and a rich learning experience. It was rumored that many of the campers in the early years were off-season clients at the private school where Ernst was the staff psychologist.

A few years ago I was comparing summer camp experiences with my friend Bill Morancy, who recalled acting in some plays at his camp. He stared at me in amazement when I told him that as an eleven-year-old, I had been in my own camp's production of Shirley Jackson's *The Lottery*. Jackson's macabre tale, first a controversial *New Yorker* short story and

Ernst and Ilse Bulova, the founders of Buck's Rock.

then a play, took place in a rural community in which the villagers come together annually, in an apparently social atmosphere, to hold a lottery. The shocking climax reveals that the "winner" will be ritually stoned to death. This might seem an odd choice of production for a teenage summer camp. But all I knew at the time was while the teens portrayed the adults, they needed a kid to play a kid, one of the youngest villagers throwing papier-mâché rocks. After Bill had regained his composure, he said, "Holy shit, what kind of camp did you go to?"

It was a camp where, in addition to *The Lottery*, the plays included Karel Čapek's *The Insect Comedy*, Jean Giraudoux's *The Madwoman of Chaillot*, and Berthold Brecht's *The Good Woman of Setzuan*. For that last one I also played a kid, a poor one with a brief moment on stage alone, rummaging through a garbage can for food. (For verisimilitude, the director made sure there was a piece of ham wrapped up in there.) The Brecht play's last rehearsals were past my bedtime, and the job of making sure I didn't fall asleep fell to an older camper, Jim McBride. About twelve years later, as a senior in college, I got to say hello to Jim again; he was premiering his influential independent film *David Holtzman's Diary* at the San Francisco Film Festival.

Jim wasn't the only camper who later became involved in films. The list (just from the years I was there) includes actress Janet Margolin,

David Holzman's Diary, a groundbreaking independent film by camp alumnus Jim McBride.

cinematographer Tom Hurwitz, director Jonathan Kaplan, screenwriter Dan Opatoshu, and film editors Paul Hirsch, Tom Bellfort, Rick Shaine, and Ron Roose.

Buck's Rock was also a place where the weekly movies included *The Life of Emile Zola, The Bicycle Thieves, Pinky* (considered daring when it came out in 1949 for its treatment of racial issues, but cringe-inducing today), and, memorably for me, *O. Henry's Full House.* Twentieth Century Fox produced this compendium film in 1952,

The Bicycle Thieves: My introduction to Italian neo-realism.

presenting five O. Henry stories, each with a different director and cast. "The Gift of the Magi" and "The Last Leaf" episodes especially affected me. I had already been conditioned, by most of the films I'd seen, to expect happy endings. Here, each story had an unexpected, ironic ending in which the characters only "sort of" lived happily ever after.

As refugees from Central Europe, the Bulovas made sure to show films about the struggle against Hitler, such as *The Seventh Cross,* with Spencer Tracy as a very unlikely German anti-Nazi who has escaped from a concentration camp.[4] But the World War II film that touched me the most was one that was actually shot at Buck's Rock itself in 1946 and shown every summer in the early fifties. The fifteen-minute film, titled *Their Voices Rise,* was narrated by the actor Francis Lederer, who knew

---

[4] "Hopelessly ill-qualified for the part," wrote James Agee in *The Nation* in 1944.

the Bulovas from their days in Berlin, when he was "Franz" Lederer. The film followed three refugee children (all played by campers) as they are welcomed warmly at Buck's Rock. When some insensitive campers play a war game with a pretend cannon, the refugee children are traumatized once more. They smash the cannon and run off into the woods. When they are found after a search, the campers apologize; chastened, they make amends by starting a food drive for the children of Europe. This short film may well have been my introduction to the physical and emotional devastation caused by the war that had ended just seven or eight years before my first viewing.

Not all the short subjects had such grave themes. Sometimes, if the evening activities were rained out, several ten- and twenty-minute films were shown in the Social Hall. It's here that I first met the animated icons Mr. Magoo and Gerald McBoing-Boing, and admired the talents of Norman McLaren and other National Film Board of Canada artists. These gifted filmmakers played with color and movement, showing me that creative animation transcended the boundaries of "cartoons."

During this time, I was a very indulged "counselor kid" and often had the run of the print and publications area (where Julia was counselor), the stage, and sometimes the camp office, where the film catalogs were stored. What a discovery that was—

Grant Munro's and Norman MacLaren's *Neighbours.*

seeing in one place the titles and descriptions of hundreds of films, with lists of stars and awards. Here I made the connection between what I was seeing on the page and what showed up on the camp screen. I thought of those moments years later when establishing the Lightning Ridge Film Society in Vermont and poring over the catalogs of Brandon Films, United Artists, Films Incorporated, and Kit Parker.

Each year the annual yearbook came out a week before camp's end. Spending time at the print and publications shop, I was a fly on the wall for the entire process: the first discussion of the theme of the yearbook, the assignment of articles, the editing of those articles into a rough draft, the collection of artwork and photos that would accompany the article, the production of a "dummy" issue, the silk-screening of the cover, then—a thrilling day!—the collation of the final product in the Social Hall. I thought of that yearbook undertaking many years later when it was time to produce the program for the Green Mountain Film Festival in Montpelier, often a daunting task with many elements. I recalled my kid's-eye view at the print shop and how I absorbed the lesson that, with patience, organization, and teamwork, an idea could incrementally become reality in six or seven weeks.

As I got older and graduated from "counselor kid" to a camper on my own, Buck's Rock provided another kind of film education. The summer I turned fourteen, my circle of friends included the children of creative filmmakers who had fallen victim to the Red Scare. Although I knew vaguely that my own parents had been in political trouble during the early 1950s, I gained a new understanding of what they experienced after hearing stories from Jonathan, Dan, and Tom about the workings of the Hollywood blacklist and how it affected their families. After camp that summer, I was finally able to ask my parents specific questions about the trauma of what was known as "the purge" of the New York City Teachers' Union.

That summer of 1961 sparked a lifelong interest in the effects of the Red Scare, both inside and outside Hollywood. Once I returned home, I started reading everything I could about the "Hollywood Ten" and the blacklist, starting with John Cogley's *Report on Blacklisting* for the Fund for the Republic, an offshoot of the Ford Foundation.[5]

Few if any of my fourteen-year-old contemporaries back in Yonkers shared my fascination with the blacklist. In fact, I doubt that anyone else in my tenth-grade class could name each member of the "Hollywood Ten" as well as the Yankees' starting lineup.

---

[5]My interest in this terrible era in American history culminated in a book, *Red Scare in the Green Mountains: Vermont in the McCarthy Era 1946–1960* (Rootstock Publishing, 2018).

◼ TRAILER:
MILLION DOLLAR LEGS

Some of the campers at Buck's Rock had family connections in the film distribution world. This meant that on occasion the camp had access to some old classics, from the silent era (before the late 1920s) or the 1930s. That's how one evening I first saw a little-known comedy with W.C. Fields called *Million Dollar Legs*. Ernie Kovacs and the Marx Brothers had already sharpened my taste for humor with a touch of the surreal, so I was a receptive audience for this zany 1932 film.

The film's release was timed for the Olympics, held in Los Angeles that year. Fields plays the president of an imaginary republic called Klopstokia, where all the inhabitants are naturally gifted athletes—hence the "legs" of the title. The men are all named George and the women Angela ("Why not?" someone offers). Migg Tweeny (Jack Oakie), a stranded traveling brush salesman, falls in love with the president's daughter Angela, played by Susan Fleming. To win her father's favor (and to put Klopstokia on the map), Migg recruits a team that will be sure to win at every event in the Olympics.

The bad girl to Susan Fleming's heroine was the femme fatale named Mata Machree, played by Lyda Roberti. The sign on the irresistible Mata Machree's door reads, "Not Responsible for Men Left After 30 Days." This character's name was both a clever nod to the Irish folk song "Mother Machree" and a knowing reference to Greta Garbo's portrayal of the notorious spy in the 1931 film *Mata Hari*. It was only many years later that I understood the Irish reference or the erotic implications of Mata's torch song, "When I Get Hot in Klopstokia." That song might not have gotten past the censors just a year later in 1933, when the prudish Production Code was enforced in Hollywood: "It's terrific when I get mean / I'm just a woman made of gelatine / I have a torso like a tambourine / Oy oy oy, when I get hot!"

The other song in the film was much tamer—and catchier. First Angela teaches Migg the traditional "Klopstokian Love Song" (gibberish set to the tune of the popular song "One Hour With You"), and later Migg serenades her. The song so impressed certain counselors at Buck's Rock that they gathered after lights-out and rescreened the entire movie, painstakingly copying the words. The lyrics were distributed at breakfast the next morning, and for a week it seemed like the whole camp was singing:

> *Woof bloogle jig*
> *Mow jig bloogle woof*
> *Oof wiggle pik*
> *Mow jig bloogle poof*
> *Wee pok pok shining*
> *Wee pok silver lining*
> *Just for you . . .*

CHAPTER 4

COMING OF AGE IN "THE HEROIC AGE"

Every time I see three-by-five lined index cards, I am transported back to my tenth-grade English class. Mrs. Beale instructed us to use those cards as an organizational aid for our oral book reports. The book I chose was Arthur Knight's *The Liveliest Art,* a comprehensive history of motion pictures. Looking back, this choice said a lot about my growing interest in learning about a larger context for the movies I so enjoyed.

Knight was the film critic for the *Saturday Review of Literature* when he wrote his influential book in 1957. The paperback copy, which appeared in 1959, was a present from my parents. As usual, they encouraged the passions of my two brothers and me, no matter how unconventional.

The Liveliest Art was my first exposure to a coherent narrative of film history. For my report, each index card represented a different era: silent film giving way to sound;

Arthur Knight's seminal book was the subject of my 10th grade book report.

the heyday of the early sound era in Hollywood with its representative genres (such as musicals, war films, gangster films, etc.); the post–World War II crisis, created by the emergence of television; and the antitrust ruling that put an end to the monopoly that was the lifeblood of the Hollywood studio system. (My classmate Greg, a car nerd just as I was a film nerd, prepared a report on Henry Ford and as an adult became a designer of racing car engines.)

My copy of *The Liveliest Art* still sits on my reference shelf, tucked between Sergei Eisenstein's *Film Form* and Pauline Kael's *I Lost It at the Movies*. Nearby is another influential book I discovered during my teenage years: Parker Tyler's *Classics of the Foreign Film*. Tyler's 1962 book, copiously illustrated with film stills, devoted an extensive essay to each of 75 films, from The *Cabinet of Dr. Caligari* (1919) to Michelangelo Antonioni's *La Notte* (1961). I discovered later that Tyler was a poet and novelist as well as a critic, an out gay man who wrote the first book about homosexuality and film, *Screening the Sexes*. At the time, all I knew was that he wrote with a passion so persuasive I wanted to see every film on his list. By my last count, I still have twenty-three to go.

I'm still working on Parker Tyler's list.

My timing couldn't have been better for developing a broader sense of film history. Excursions to the movies were no longer solely with my parents; I was finally old enough to take the bus and subway into Manhattan, where repertory houses like the New Yorker, Thalia, and Bleecker Street Cinema provided a steady stream of films from the 1940s and earlier. With my high school and summer camp friends—and sometimes on my own—I experienced the variety of venues in Manhattan, from the barely functioning Charles Theater in the East Village to the high-class Coronet and Baronet, both right across Third Avenue from Bloomingdale's.

My burgeoning fascination came at a time when there was, according to writer Phillip Lopate, "a phenomenal period of cinematic creativity." In his 1998 essay "Anticipation of *La Notte*," Lopate referred to the years from the late 1950s to the mid-1960s as "the Heroic Age of Moviegoing." It seemed that every week a new film by the likes of François Truffaut, Ingmar Bergman, Federico Fellini, or Andrzej Wajda opened in New York.

One of my teenage haunts.

Films like *A Taste of Honey* explored teenage pregnancy, homosexuality, and racial issues, while comedies such as *Divorce, Italian Style* were far from the Hollywood standards of good taste. But the films that attracted me most went even deeper. I loved the sense of immersion in a foreign worldview that the enigmatic films of that era provided. So many of them, it seemed, had ambiguous endings that left my friends and me discussing the film for hours: Ingmar Bergman's *Wild Strawberries*, Antonioni's *L'Eclisse*, and Roman Polanski's *Knife in the Water* come immediately to mind.

•

Here I must pay tribute to some people, then unknown to me by name, who provided me with many hours of pleasure and education:

• Ursula Lewis, who owned and operated the tiny and uncomfortable but vital Thalia Theater on 95th Street near Broadway.

• Rudy Franchi, who booked amazing double and triple bills at the Bleecker Street Cinema (one I sat through paired *Citizen Kane* and *The Magnificent Ambersons,* both by Orson Welles, with Kenzo Mizogushi's *Ugetsu* in between).

• Dan and Toby Talbot, the couple who operated the New Yorker Theater on Broadway at 88th Street.

• Donald Rugoff, who booked the Rugoff chain of art house cinemas that included the Beekman, the Sutton, the Art, the Fifth Street Playhouse, the Gramercy, and eventually the flagship Cinema I and Cinema II, on the same block as the Coronet and Baronet.

•

The New Yorker film critic Anthony Lane paid tribute to Rugoff, reviewing Ira Deutchman's 2021 documentary *Searching for Mr. Rugoff.* Lane said, "If you are a New Yorker with catholic appetites and a long memory, it may well be that your life was shaped by Donald S. Rugoff, though his name will ring no bells. Back in the day, whenever you took your seat at a movie theatre like the Plaza, the Paris, the Beekman, or the Sutton, you were entering the realm of Rugoff . . . probably the greatest distributor of independent and art films in the nineteen-sixties and nineteen-seventies."

Someone in Rugoff's office, perhaps the man himself, had the idea to make discount tickets to all his theaters available to New York City high school students. It was "a gala day" (as Margaret Dumont said to Groucho) every time my mother periodically brought home these tickets from the High School of Music and Art, where she taught. Here are just a few of the films that were showing at the Rugoff theaters when I was a senior in high school in 1964–1965: Jean-Luc Godard's *A Married Woman;* René Clément's *Purple Noon,* an adaptation of Patricia Highsmith's *The Talented Mr. Ripley;* Sidney Lumet's *The Hill,* with Sean Connery breaking out of his James Bond mold in a tough prison drama; Tony Richardson's wild comedy *The Loved One;* John Schlesinger's very hip, up-to-the-minute *Darling;* and Richard Lester's Beatles film *Help!*

My favorite haunt during my high school and college years was the Talbots' New Yorker Theater, formerly a "picture palace" called the Yorktown. The Talbots took over the management in 1960 and the theater, with its carved ceiling and red velvet walls, quickly became a magnet for cinephiles. Toby Talbot, in her recent memoir about operating the theater, might have been speaking specifically of me when she wrote, "Most of our audience were ordinary moviegoers wanting to dream and feel the breath of others. The theater served as a barometer to critical and popular taste and helped to shape the taste of a new generation." An indication of the Talbots' success is that several of the films in their 1961 "Forgotten Film" series—*White Heat, Bringing Up Baby, High Sierra,* and *The Big Sleep*—are now anything but forgotten.

I became a regular at their W.C. Fields and Marx Brothers retrospectives. And I couldn't leave the theater without a glance at the ledger book at the rear section where patrons signed up for the mailing list and made suggestions of what they wanted the theater to show. Those eclectic suggestions served as a recommendation list for me as well as for the Talbots.

Thus exposed to the classics of the 1930s and 1940s at the New Yorker, I became aware of the truth of Andrew Sarris' dictum that the glory of cinema is that it simultaneously belongs to each of us individually as well as to the audience as a whole. Many years later, I thought about those hours spent at the New Yorker and other theaters when I had the opportunity to create the Savoy Theater—my own magnet for cinephiles in Montpelier, Vermont.

I first saw *The Cabinet of Dr. Caligari,* a classic, at the Thalia.

▣ TRAILER:
CHILDREN OF PARADISE

There were several films selected by Parker Tyler in his *Classics of the Foreign Film* that went to the top of my wish list. One was *Les Enfants du Paradis*, a French film better known in the United States as *Children of Paradise*. In his characteristically luxuriant style, Tyler wrote, "It has the opulence that comes only with worldly experience, the feeling that men and women—and only men and women—have created the world of health and joy, grief, mishap, disaster and revelation that entwines them and utters their direction as if from a stage." Those were heady words for someone who didn't have any worldly experience yet, but they certainly made me eager to see for myself what Tyler may have meant.

Fortunately, living near Manhattan meant that I was bound to have a chance to see the film, at either the Bleecker Street Cinema, the Thalia, or the New Yorker. It immediately became a touchstone for me. I was fascinated by the milieu (the theater world of 1830s Paris) and moved by the full-bodied characters and their deeply romantic story. It's a three-hour film that I'm always sorry to see end.

Children of Paradise: like a nineteenth century novel.

The film's title refers to the impoverished audience members who could only afford a seat in the Théâtre des Funambules's upper balcony. The writer Jacques Prévert, already widely known as a poet, created a story involving well-known figures of the time: the mime Baptiste Deburau, the actor Frédérick Lemâitre, the criminal Pierre-François Lacenaire, and the wealthy Count Édouard de Montray (based on the Duc de Morny).

There is no historical proof that any of these people were acquainted with each other. It was Prévert's inspiration that not only did they know each other, but that they were all in love with the same (fictional) woman, Garance.

The more I discovered about this film, the more fascinating it became. Marcel Carné, the director, shot the film in 1943 and 1944, during and after the German occupation. Even though it is set a hundred years in the past, Prévert and Carné were very much aware that they were making a political statement. Carné said in a 1975 interview, "We tried to regain through the spirit what had been lost by the sword." The film is, among its many virtues, a stirring tribute to French love of the arts and exhibits a deep respect for France's cultural history.

It's hard to imagine a film, especially a spectacular

A contemporary drawing of the Théâtre des Funambules.

costume drama, being produced under such stressful conditions. There were undercover agents of the French Resistance among the 1,800 extras at the Victorian Studios in Nice, using the film shoot as cover. Carné also had to avoid antagonizing pro-Nazi collaborators and Vichy sympathizers placed on the production by the authorities.[6] After Paris was liberated in August 1944, midway through the filming, one supporting actor, Robert Le Vigan, was sentenced to death by the Resistance as a Nazi collaborator; all his scenes as the ragman Jéricho were reshot, now with Pierre Renoir in the role.[7]

Two major creative contributors to the film, composer Joseph Kosma and production designer Alexandre Trauner, were Jewish, so they had to work on the film in secret. In the restored version, they are listed in the credits

---

[6]Nice, where most of the film was shot, was in the southern third of France controlled by the pro-Nazi government headquartered in Vichy.

[7]In 1946, Le Vigan's sentence was commuted to ten years at hard labor. He was released on parole after three years, but fled to Spain and then Argentina, where he died in 1972.

as *collaborateurs clandestinés*. In a 1982 interview, Trauner recalled that he might have had a chance to leave France, but chose to stay, albeit in hiding, because he was so attached to his friends in the industry. "It was my world," he said.

Although the film has a richness I associate with nineteenth century novels, its twentieth century historical context gave the film an added dimension. Seeing the film in the 1960s and 1970s, though, was frustrating in two ways: perhaps only half of Prévert's sublime dialogue was actually subtitled on screen, and those subtitles were often hard to read. The scenes with Lacenaire were especially difficult, featuring white subtitles on the white ruffled shirt he wore continuously throughout the film.

After one showing of the film at the Savoy in the late 1980s, I conceived the idea for a coffee-table book on the film. It would contain a full translation of Prévert's script, background information on the making of the film, critical essays, and short biographies of the film's glorious cast: the real-life mime Jean-Louis Barrault as Baptiste (in a performance that was, said James Agee, the "only depiction, on screen, of an artist, which has fully convinced me of the genius he was supposed to have"); Pierre Brasseur as the vainglorious actor Frédérick; Marcel Herrand as the villainous Lacenaire; and Arletty as the elusive and desirable Garance.

My wife, Andrea, and I had long dreamed of a trip to France. In the spring of 1992, we combined pleasure with film research. Our good friend Bill Durkee, a Montpelier native and longtime Paris resident, arranged appointments for us at photo archives and museums. There was always a scenic route to get to these places—through the Tuileries, over the Pont Neuf, or past the Place Vendôme. What a way to see Paris! With Bill acting as our translator, I amassed a trove of contemporaneous documents, clippings, and photos.

The high point was an afternoon at the Musée Carnavalet, the museum of the city of Paris. The museum curator gave us white cotton gloves, and we examined the very contract that Baptiste Deburau signed with the Théâtre des Funambules, where the film's action takes place. We saw the newspapers that announced the death of Frédérick Lemâitre in 1876 and the conviction of Pierre-François Lacenaire for murder in 1836.

As the characters in the film might say, *Hélas!* Nothing ever came of my project. It was too general for a university press and too specialized for other publishers. The mention of this film—a talisman for so many of my art house generation—drew blank stares. It seemed that many in the publishing world were too young to have my magical connection to the film. The potential costs of intercontinental permissions for photos and text also promised to be prohibitive.

Much of what I envisioned for this comprehensive book did come to pass years later, in the form of a two-DVD set from the Criterion Collection. In this restored version, the subtitles were more complete (revealing the subtlety of Prévert's poetic language) and also, finally, readable. Hours of supplements on the Criterion discs filled out much of the film's complex history.

Every few years, either Andrea or I will ask, "Time for *Children of Paradise* again?" We'll rent the Savoy and spread the word. Some in the audience have been waiting for a chance to see it for the first time, or for their first time since college, or to come back for their fifth round. Some have come reluctantly, giving in to their partners' admonition: "You have to see this movie!" We hope they leave the theater feeling as we do: that this is an epic that fulfills the potential of cinema to transport us to another century, another country, and another culture—altogether another reality.

CHAPTER 5

THANK YOU, SCHOOL OF VISUAL ARTS

A notice on the bulletin board at the High School of Music and Art provided the catalyst for my first—and only—film appreciation class. And what an enlightening class it was. In the spring of 1964, my mother, Julia, saw the notice outside her art classroom and wondered if I would be interested in taking this course. It would meet each Monday night during the summer at the School of Visual Arts (SVA) on 23rd Street in Manhattan. I didn't have to think about it, even though I had no idea who would be teaching the course and I knew that in all likelihood I would be the youngest enrollee.

I didn't know anything about SVA: how it began in 1947 as the Cartoonists and Illustrators School or how the visionary educator Silas Rhodes turned it into the School of Visual Arts in 1956. The school's website credits Rhodes with "reflecting a belief that there is more to art than technique, and that learning to become an artist is not the same as learning a trade."

Rhodes was still running the school in 1964. Earlier that year he had worked with the illustrator/filmmaker/graphic designer Everett Aison to start the SVA Film School. One of Aison's first acts as department head was to hire the renowned (though unknown to me at the time) film historian William K. Everson, who co-taught that summer class with Aison. How lucky I was: two accomplished figures in the film world would be my instructors.

In the days before video, Everson's screenings of lost or forgotten Hollywood films helped educate film buffs and professionals alike. His *New York Times* obituary of 1994 said that "his role in American film culture has been compared to that of Henri Langlois, the founder of the Cinémathèque Française, in France." Kevin Brownlow, a noted film historian himself,

Erudite film maven, William K. Everson.

paid tribute to Everson in an obituary in *The Independent,* where he called Everson: "a popularist, rather than an academic, responsible for many books, hundreds of articles and thousands of program notes—but above all, he loved teaching. . . . He was a brilliant teacher. I have often sat in on his lectures and wished that I could recall exactly what he said and how he said it."

I, too, wish I could revisit those classes. I do remember Everson's demeanor, though. He was perhaps the most serious and formal person I had yet observed in my sixteen years. An expatriate Brit, he looked to be well beyond his thirty-seven years. He seemed to have stepped out of a British novel or one of writer/illustrator Edward Gorey's Victorian mansions. Indeed, a 2018 *New Yorker* article on Gorey mentioned that the author of *The Gashlycrumb Tinies* and other darkly humorous works had been a regular visitor to Everson's apartment, where an informal film club gathered to see gems from Everson's vast collection of films in sixteen-millimeter format.

Aison, just thirty at the time of the class, frequently deferred to Everson, but he had an expert eye as well. He had already designed the iconic posters for the American premieres of Louis Malle's *Zazie Dans Le Métro* (1960), Akira Kurosawa's *Yojimbo* (1961), and Roman Polanski's *Knife in the Water* (1963).

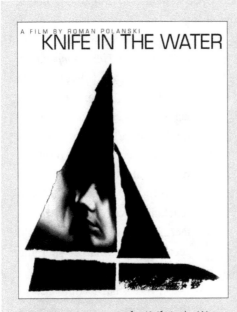

Everett Aison's poster art for *Knife in the Water.*

In his creative career, he directed several short films, illustrated children's books, and wrote *Artrage,* a satire of the art world. He was a mainstay of the SVA faculty until his retirement.

I reconnected with Everett Aison in 2018, fifty-four years after that summer course. I found he was eager to reminisce about the class and to share his respect for Bill Everson's encyclopedic knowledge of and passion for film. "I know we saw F.W. Murnau's silent classic *Sunrise* and Sergei Eisenstein's *Potemkin*," I recalled. "What else would have been on that curriculum?" "Well, there certainly would have been a Chaplin and a Keaton.... and probably Jean Renoir's *La Grande Illusion*," Aison said. "And Bill loved John Ford's westerns, so very likely *My Darling Clementine.*"

One evening stood out, but not for anything Aison and Everson did, besides direct us to the auditorium. Critic Andrew Sarris, who was about to join the SVA faculty, was to show and discuss Alfred Hitchcock's *Shadow of a Doubt.* This was deemed by Aison and Everson worth forgoing a class. I had already been reading Sarris' film reviews in the *Village Voice* whenever I could, so it was a thrill to hear this perceptive and iconoclastic critic offer his insights. His influence continued to grow in the years since 1964. When Sarris died in 2012, film historian David Bordwell

Jean Renoir's *La Grande Illusion* was one of the films I saw that summer.

wrote on his *Observations on Film Art* blog, "Sarris' death reminds us how much American culture can owe to a single person."

That night, Sarris shared his enthusiasm for the film and his appreciation of Hitchcock's techniques. He alerted us to various motifs we should watch for: the double (the evil Uncle Charlie and his innocent niece, "Young Charlie"), the evil lurking under a placid exterior (in this case Santa Rosa, California), and Hitchcock's ever-present preoccupation with guilt and innocence. Speaking about Joseph Cotten's villainous Uncle Charlie, Sarris pointed out something that I've since stressed in my own film lectures: Hitchcock believed that the more vivid the villain, the more successful the picture will be.[8]

•

That one evening in 1964 at the School of Visual Arts came to have resonance forty years later. In 2004, Sarris' wife, the critic and author Molly Haskell, was our guest at the Green Mountain Film Festival in Montpelier. She loved Montpelier and the intimacy of our festival, but she was concerned about having left Andrew at home. He was

---

[8]Some examples: Mrs. Danvers (Judith Anderson) in *Rebecca,* Alexander Sebastian (Claude Rains) in *Notorious,* and Bruno Anthony (Robert Walker) in *Strangers on a Train.*

Teresa Wright and Joseph Cotten in *Shadow of a Doubt.*

in declining health, and Molly called him several times a day. But as Molly told me, the calls weren't just about his health. He told her which movies he was watching and as Molly said with a laugh and a roll of her eyes, "what beautiful new actresses he had just discovered." When I said goodbye at the end of her stay, I told her what an influence her husband had been on my life. Ever the gracious southerner, Molly said, "Well, next time you're in New York, come tell him yourself."

It took a few years, but in 2010, my wife Andrea and I did spend a few hours at the Sarris-Haskell apartment. We were slightly nervous about meeting such a giant of film criticism, but we needn't have worried. Andrew immediately asked Andrea what her favorite Hitchcock film was; when she named *Shadow of a Doubt*, all the ice was broken. Andrew didn't remember the lecture at SVA so many years earlier, but he confirmed that the film was his own favorite Hitchcock. He then devoted all his rapt attention to Andrea, who had convincingly established her bona fides.

Molly and I chatted about her new book, *Frankly, My Dear*, an examination of her own complex feelings (as a Southern belle manqué) toward *Gone With the Wind*. Andrew regaled us with stories of his so-called feud with the acerbic critic Pauline Kael.

The disagreement with Kael, which played out in the pages of small but influential film magazines, nevertheless had ripple effects in the community of film critics and scholars. The source of controversy was the auteur theory, which was first put forth by the French critics associated with the prestigious magazine *Cahiers du Cinema*. To simplify (greatly), *Cahiers* critics like André Bazin and the young François Truffaut viewed the director as the major creative force in a motion picture. This may be a given in today's movie world, but the French critics were the first to bring attention to some neglected American directors. They argued that Howard Hawks and Raoul Walsh, for example, were able to put a certain stamp of personality on studio-assigned pictures. Among American film critics, Sarris was perhaps the foremost champion of this then-innovative approach to perceiving how films are conceived and realized. But in the pages of *Film Quarterly* in 1963, Kael attacked the auteur theory at length and Sarris in particular. "Sarris, who thinks he is applying a single theory, is too undisciplined to recognize the conflicting implications of his arguments," she wrote. All these years later, Sarris remained perplexed why Kael brought such personal vitriol to their disagreement. He had expected a collegial discourse between two people passionately devoted to film. "All the feuding," Andrew said, "was on her side."

We had enjoyed a memorable and scintillating few hours with Andrew and Molly, and as our visit drew to an end, we dreaded going out into the pouring rain. Andrew, with genuine courtliness, helped Andrea on with her coat and for good measure kissed her hand. Our heads were spinning when we got to the elevator, as though we had consumed a magnum of champagne.

CHAPTER 6

TWO CAMPUSES, TWO UPHEAVALS

As a result of being the editor-in-chief of my high school paper, *The Scroll,* I was able to attend the Interscholastic Press Association conference, held each year at Columbia University. As soon as I stepped onto the campus that spring day in 1964, I knew that Columbia would be my first choice for college. In addition to breathing the intellectually charged air of an Ivy League school, I was immediately struck by the visible evidence of the Vietnam War protest. Tables with antiwar information were prominent on Low Plaza. I witnessed heated discussions between antiwar activists and dissenting students. In this heady atmosphere, all the ferment of the 1960s (which hadn't reached my suburban high school yet) was palpable.

I also looked forward to living in—rather than visiting—Manhattan. No more would I have to call my parents to arrange a ride from the terminus of the D train, the Lexington line, or the #1 Broadway (a.k.a. "the slow boat to China"). The Thalia and the New Yorker, as well as the Midtown on 100th Street, would be a long walk or a short bus ride away.

When I did enter Columbia College, in the fall of 1965, I discovered that I didn't even have to leave campus to see films. Several film societies were active, inviting luminaries like Paul Newman and Eli Wallach to appear with their films. There were Italian films at the Casa Italiana and French ones at the Alliance Française. But the main draw was still off-campus, and my most vivid moviegoing memories from those days involve group outings to the New Yorker for a W.C. Fields festival and a ride down to the Village to the Bleecker Street Cinema.[9] On one occasion, the Bleecker showed two Jean Cocteau films, *Orpheus* and *Beauty and the Beast*. I didn't think I'd seen *Beauty and the Beast* before. But when the arms holding candelabras protruded from the wall of the Beast's castle, I knew that I had seen the Cocteau film many years before, on television.

By my junior year, the thrill of being in Manhattan had waned. Although I had some excellent instructors, the idea of academia, too, lost its luster. I knew that I was not a good candidate for graduate school. I had neither the ambition to succeed, an overwhelming passion for one course of study, or the requisite zitsfleysh (in Yiddish, literally "sitting flesh," or assiduous concentration). Plus it was 1967: the prospect of hours in the library paled next to the siren call of an antiwar protest or a Paul Butterfield Blues Band concert or a "be-in" in Central Park.

Social life at Columbia was difficult, as well. Many of my friends had paired off, and I discovered how lonely a place Columbia could be. Though Barnard College, Columbia's sister school, was right across Broadway, I was too diffident to take any initiative. (As my friend Bob Rosenfeld likes to say, "I never got the manual.")

I began to think seriously about leaving Columbia. During the summer of 1967, word had filtered back to New York about San Francisco's "Summer of Love" and the flowering of an active counter-culture in the Bay Area. The two weeks between the end of a summer job and the start of school were an ideal time to visit friends in Berkeley. It was my first trip to California, and I was stunned. So much sunshine, and no subways! Lemons on the trees! Driving to the redwoods or the Pacific! A free Grateful Dead concert! Before the two weeks were over, I was mulling a plan to transfer to UC Berkeley.

With the tumultuous events of the spring of 1968, my transfer application, submitted the previous fall, hit a major stumbling block: the student occupation of several buildings at Columbia. There were

---

[9]When I saw my Columbia classmate Paul Auster again after a thirty-year hiatus, his first words were, "You were the one who told me about rear projection." That is the technique in which the actors sit in the car and the scenery goes by around them, so I must already have had some working knowledge of how films are made.

two major issues that roiled the campus that April and May: race (the University's questionable decision to build a new gymnasium in Morningside Park, which bordered Harlem) and the Vietnam War (the discovery of the University's secret partnership with the Pentagon-supported Institute for Defense Analyses). Several buildings were occupied for a week, and classes were suspended for the rest of the year.

April, 1968: Tearing down the gym construction site fence.

Meanwhile, I received an official letter from Berkeley: my grades were just shy of the 3.0 grade point average required for acceptance. However, the admissions office would wait until my spring grades were in before making a final decision. But with the suspension of classes at Columbia there would be no spring grades. What to do? I decided to approach each of my professors individually and request a letter saying "If we had completed classes, I would have given him . . . " With the help of sympathetic instructors like David Rosand (an A in Art History) and Edward Tayler (an A+ in Elizabethan Literature!), I was on my way to Berkeley by June.

•

It was a surprise to learn that Berkeley had an even more active film culture than Columbia. If I had done my Berkeley history homework, I would have known that Pauline Kael, Ernest Callenbach, and Edward

Landberg had been at the center of a lively film scene there throughout the 1950s and 1960s. The Cinema-Guild theater, which they helped found, still stood in downtown Berkeley.

Just a block from campus was the Northside Theater, named for that extremely hilly neighborhood. Whoever programmed that theater had a fondness for the French New Wave, and that is where I caught up with many films I had missed in New York (like Jean-Luc Godard's *Vivre Sa Vie*). There I also laughed as loud as I ever had in a theater, seeing Woody Allen's *What's Up, Tiger Lily?* Allen had bought the rights to a low-grade Japanese spy movie and redubbed it in English. Now with a plot involving a secret recipe for chicken salad, it featured such lines as "I'd call him a sadistic, bestial necrophile, but that would be beating a dead horse."

The theater where I spent the most time was right off campus on Telegraph Avenue. Tom Luddy and others had just founded the Telegraph Repertory Cinema. In 1971, this venture became part of the impressive Pacific Film Archive, a few blocks away. But in its original incarnation

TELEGRAPH Repertory Cinema
Tel.&Dwt.848-8650
Cinema I: Two Private Eye Greats
R. Chandler's "Murder My Sweet"
Humphrey Bogart "Maltese Falcon"
Murder 6:30, 9:45-Falcon 8:05, 11:20
Cinema II: World Cinema Repertory
Luis Bunuel's "LOS OLVIDADOS"
Bunuel's "El" ("This Strange
Passion")
Olvi. 6:30, 9:10-Strange 7:50, 10:30

A typical program at the "Telegraph Rep."

the Telegraph Rep, as it was known, was, to put it generously, funky. I quickly learned not to sit on the left side of the theater, lest the dialogue be drowned out by the all-night laundromat next door.

During the year I spent in Berkeley, there were several multi-week retrospectives at the Telegraph Rep, but I remember two in particular. The first featured many, if not all, of the films of Fritz Lang. The German-born director had been a Los Angeles resident for many years. He was scheduled to visit the UC campus in the fall of 1968, and the Telegraph Rep scheduled three weeks of Lang films to celebrate the occasion. Thus, I saw several of his silent films, plus many of the films noir that he directed after he arrived in Hollywood in 1936. I had seen one of those noirs, *The Woman in the Window,* years before, without knowing anything about either Lang or the term noir, which has since become a catch-all phrase for the black and white atmospheric films of the 1940s—often featuring a city at night, a sum of money, double- and triple-crosses, a weak-willed male protagonist, and a scheming femme fatale.

Another Lang film was *Scarlet Street*, which, like *The Woman in the Window*, starred Edward G. Robinson, Joan Bennett, and Dan Duryea. Lang's inspiration was the film *La Chienne* ("The Bitch"), directed by Jean Renoir fourteen years earlier, in 1931. It was an occasion for one of the many campus film societies—the one that showed nothing but French-language films—to show the original Renoir film. However, there was a problem: the film that arrived was an unsubtitled version. There was a frantic phone call to the University's French Department, and that evening a film-loving French professor took the microphone to provide a simultaneous translation.

Scarlet Street, Fritz Lang's remake of *La Chienne*.

The other Telegraph Rep retrospective that I remember most vividly presented three weeks of Buster Keaton features and shorts. In a 1950 essay for *The Nation*, "Comedy's Greatest Era," James Agee had written, "For pure hard laughter, the shorts were even better than the features." At the time of Agee's article, it was assumed that the negatives of these nineteen shorts (such as *The Electric House* and *One Week*) had been lost forever. But in 1954, actor James Mason moved into Keaton's former mansion and came upon a stack of film cans containing those shorts. By 1968, they were once again in circulation.

Tom Luddy and company also made a brilliant decision in presenting the Keaton films, perhaps taking their cue from Agee's description of Keaton's face as "haunting, handsome, almost beautiful."

Instead of the usual silent-film piano music, these films at the Telegraph Rep had as their accompaniment piano works by the French impressionist composer Erik Satie. Satie's whimsical, humorous, and often otherworldly music perfectly complemented the fifty-year-old films that conjured another era.

Buster Keaton in *The Electric House.*

Another Telegraph Rep memory: one night, in the midst of the notorious 1968 Democratic convention in Chicago, I left an antiwar demonstration in downtown Berkeley to catch the Howard Hawks comedy *His Girl Friday.* In one scene, an accused killer escapes from prison and hides in the newsroom where Cary Grant and Rosalind Russell are covering the story. One character bursts into the room yelling, "The place is surrounded by cops!" At that very moment, someone ran into the theater shouting the exact same message; the Berkeley police were chasing antiwar demonstrators from downtown up to the Telegraph Rep's neighborhood. The audience huddled in the theater past the end of the movie, waiting until they could safely walk out onto Telegraph Avenue again.

The political turbulence continued into the fall. My one academic year at UC Berkeley was interrupted three times by political unrest. In the fall trimester, it was the controversy over Black Panther Eldridge Cleaver guest-teaching a course called "Social Analysis 139X: Dehumanization and Regeneration of the American Social Order." The winter trimester ground to a halt when the agitation for a Third World Studies Department spread from San Francisco State across the Bay to Berkeley. The spring semester was the most fraught: the fight over People's Park (a neglected lot owned by the University and reclaimed by community activists) resulted in the death of one protester and the blinding of another one by shotgun pellets. Governor Ronald Reagan and California attorney general Edwin Meese called on the National Guard and the dreaded "Blue Meanies" (deputies of the Alameda County Sheriff's Department) to restore order and give the land back to the University.

POLICE SEIZE PARK; SHOOT AT LEAST 35

March Triggers Ave. Gassing; Bystanders, Students Wounded; Emergency, Curfew Enforced

The Daily Californian

People's Park, May 1970: a tumultuous time in Berkeley.

It was time to leave Berkeley. Less than a year after I had been first captivated by Berkeley's serenity, I was now risking arrest just by walking down the street. I took part in one more protest over the People's Park occupation, joining many others to walk out of our own graduation. I then packed up, drove cross-country with my Berkeley pal Ray Neinstein, who was moving east, and landed back at my parents' house in Yonkers in July 1969. I had no idea what was going to happen next, except for a plan to visit some old friends while waiting for my draft notice. They happened to live in Plainfield, Vermont.

▣ TRAILER:
THE TESTAMENT OF DR. MABUSE

The Telegraph Rep's Fritz Lang retrospective was an eye-opener. Lang had been an innovator during the 1920s, part of the German Expressionism movement that influenced the painting, architecture, and film of the time. The retrospective included all fourteen of Lang's silent films, including the four-and-a-half-hour crime drama from 1923, *Dr. Mabuse, the Gambler*, shown over two nights. The story of this villainous mastermind was like no other silent film I had seen; it was dark and atmospheric, compared to the airy Charlie Chaplin or Laurel and Hardy comedies I had associated with silents. I had anticipated the length would be a challenge, but Lang's paranoid vision of a German society in collapse was riveting. When it was time a week later for the next installment, Lang's 1933 film, *The Testament of Dr. Mabuse*, I was ready.

Fritz Lang did not direct the first German sound film: that was a 1929 filmed performance of the Berlin Philharmonic performing Richard Wagner's *Der Meistersinger*. But his brilliant 1931 crime drama *M* (which made an international star of Peter Lorre) established Lang as the preeminent German director of the new sound era. *M* is perhaps Lang's best-known film, a longtime requirement in many film classes. However, it was his second sound film that captured my attention. Watching *The Testament of Dr. Mabuse* remains one of my most thrilling and visceral movie-going experiences.

In this sequel to the silent film made nearly a decade earlier, the mad doctor is now locked up in an asylum, but the director of the hospital has been carrying out the doctor's nefarious plots. As the film begins, we are plunged into mystery: we are in an industrial workshop and there is no dialogue, just the infernal sounds of machinery. Someone—whether a good guy or not, we don't know—is hiding there, fearing for his life. If there was ever an opening scene to capture the audience's attention, this was it.

I couldn't wait to return the next night to see it again, dragging my friend Abbie Thomson with me. I was taken with the stark visual imagery of the film, the tortuous plot, and the electrifying action sequences. There seemed to be one nail-biting climax after another. I loved how each new scene began with a freeze-frame, only to explode into motion five seconds later.

I was surprised to learn several years later that what I had seen in Berkeley was an incomplete and inferior version. The original German negative was presumed lost, a casualty of World War II. The film I saw that night had been made from a print discovered in France after the war. It was available to English-speaking audiences with dubbed dialogue—and with the addition of those freeze-frames that impressed me so much. But around the time I saw that film in Berkeley, the original print was discovered in Germany and then restored according to Lang's instructions. When that version was shown in New York in 1973, those freeze-frames had been eliminated and the film was now twenty minutes longer than the version I had seen. *New York Times* critic Nora Sayre referred to this version's "sensational torrent of images, rich in the shocks at which Lang excelled."

Cinematographer Curt Courant and director Fritz Lang (with monocle!) on the set of *Woman in the Moon* (1929).

Fritz Lang, with his steely gaze and his trademark monocle, seemed ancient when he came to the Berkeley campus in October 1970, but I see now he was barely seventy. (In the youth culture that permeated Berkeley, even forty qualified as doddering.) Lang hadn't directed a film since 1960, and, fittingly, it was one final film about the mad doctor: *The Thousand Eyes of Dr. Mabuse.* I was among a small group who heard him speak about the film's rich historical background.

He had us spellbound as he told the story of how *The Testament of Dr. Mabuse* came to the attention of Nazi propaganda minister Joseph Goebbels. Though the film could be read as an anti-Nazi parable (with lines of Nazi propaganda coming out of the mouths of criminals), Goebbels was sufficiently impressed by the artistry that he offered Lang the job as head of the German film industry.

Lang conjured up the scene in Goebbels' office. The sweat was trickling down his back as he nervously looked through the window at a clock across the way. He had to figure out how much time he had to get to the bank, withdraw his savings, and take the first train to Paris. Once he was safely gone, the Nazis took the film out of circulation, calling it an "incitement to public disorder."

It was a very exciting story, but not exactly true, as I found out much later. According to Lang biographer Patrick McGilligan, he had been polishing that tale for years. As a director of thrillers, he knew how to hold an audience in his thrall. The film was indeed banned, but it was a full four months before Lang went to Paris to stay (after a year there, he went to Hollywood). No matter: I won't soon forget that afternoon in Lang's presence.[10]

---

[10]There was an amusing postscript to my immersion in Lang's films. His appearance on campus was in October 1968, and I was planning to spend that Thanksgiving break in Los Angeles with old friends of my parents, Bee and Ed Goodlaw. But shortly before this trip, I had a dream that it was Fritz Lang who would be my host in Los Angeles: he had already made plans to show me around. I related this dream to the Goodlaws when I got to their house—only to discover that Ed Goodlaw was Lang's optometrist, the one responsible for maintaining the director's supply of monocles!

2008 Green Mountain Film Festival cover art by Thea Alvin.

PART 2

PUTTING DOWN ROOTS
1970-1980

CHAPTER 7

ARRIVING AT "THE CENTER OF THE UNIVERSE"

The index card on the bulletin board at Goddard College had a simple message: "House and 30 acres, organic garden, five minutes from Plainfield." I saw the notice within a half-hour of my arrival during the last week of August 1970. The next day I saw the property, and within a week my parents had come to Vermont and bought it—for a rock-bottom price that was possible in those years. It was just before the completion of Interstates 89 and 91 transformed Vermont, bringing skiers, second-home purchasers, and young "urban refugees" in large numbers, sending property values soaring.

I'm still stunned at the leap of faith my parents, Julia and Leon, took. My brother Jon and I absorbed the "back-to-the-land" spirit that abounded in our generation of urban and suburban youth in the late 1960s. We had both been enthusiastic about the possibility of moving to a rural environment, but the speed at which it happened left me dizzy. I had grown up in the suburbs, spent three years in New York City, one year in the never-never land of a college town in California—and now I was living in a rural "needs work" house, two miles up a dirt road from Route 14. I was also without the job at Goddard that I had hoped to begin.

Earlier that spring I had made my brief first trip to Vermont to visit friends from Buck's Rock, the summer camp of my youth.[11] But before

---

[11]This was directly after receiving a draft deferment, leaving me free to make plans.

I landed at the "old Orr place," seen here circa 1940.

leaving New York I had one of those chance encounters that set the stage for everything to come. I had run into a Columbia acquaintance who had spent some time in Middlebury, Vermont. "If you're ever in Plainfield," he said, "be sure to look up my friend Walter Ungerer, who's running the film program at Goddard."

I did meet Walter, and the two of us had an immediate rapport. I learned that the so-called "film program" was just him. Walter, who in subsequent years went on to make several well-regarded independent films such as *The House Without Steps*, was looking for an assistant. He had an ambitious idea: to put Goddard College on the map as a repository for "underground" films, independent films, and student films. Walter asked about my plans, and when I responded that I didn't have any, he suggested I sign on to help with his vision—pending, of course, approval by the administration.

I didn't know then that Goddard College, famous for its unconventional approach to education since its inception in 1938, was at a crucial stage in its history. It had been founded by Royce "Tim" Pitkin, who had been inspired by the bold theories of the educator John Dewey and Dewey's protégé William Heard Kilpatrick of Columbia University's Teachers College. Pitkin had attended a conference where Kilpatrick laid out principles for envisioning a progressive college, including a belief that "education must deal with the whole lives of students, and must be concerned with social and moral responsibility."

Walter Ungerer, Goddard's one-man film department.

Pitkin believed that a small Vermont community offered an ideal setting for such education. As Goddard College took shape, Pitkin himself became nationally known as an educational innovator, bringing to life Dewey's and Kilpatrick's theories about student participation in the learning process.[12] He and his colleagues at Goddard did away with the grading system, written examinations, required courses, credits, fraternities, athletics, honor rolls, and diplomas. I started hearing about the place as a teenager; several of my summer camp friends, attracted by Goddard's unorthodox, holistic approach to education, were hoping to go there.The counterculture currents of the late 1960s also put the town of Plainfield on the map as an "anything goes" destination. Plainfield was like other Vermont towns or villages, with its general store, its rough-and-tumble gas station, and its church on the village green, but the outsize influence of Goddard was in evidence, even on my short visit. Goddard graduates were staying in the area; their friends who had come to visit from urban areas liked the atmosphere and relocated there or nearby (I was about to become one of them myself). Plainfield and the

---

[12] It is no accident that two of the dorms on Goddard's Greatwood campus are named Kilpatrick and Dewey.

surrounding region was becoming an incubator for alternative institutions such as health food stores, communes, art studios, and organic farms. I also noted Plainfield's proximity to the state capital, Montpelier, fifteen minutes away—unlike more isolated rural towns in Vermont. My friend Anne Zuckerman, like me an urban emigré, wryly commented, "Plainfield is a very deceptive place: you'd never guess it is the center of the universe."

After more than thirty years as Goddard's president, Pitkin retired in 1969 and was succeeded by Gerald Witherspoon, then Vermont's tax commissioner. With his background in finance, Gerry (as he was known to everyone) was presumed to be a safe choice. The story I heard was that Gerry soon took off his Clark Kent office suit to reveal a caped educational crusader, eager to establish his own forward-looking bona fides.

New programs, like women's studies, were established. Students, under the supervision of architects John Mallery and David Sellers, designed and built the striking Design Center. The Bread and Puppet Theater, a politically engaged performance group founded by Peter and Elka Schumann, was invited to leave its home in New York City's East Village and become Goddard's theater company in residence. Those who had unsuccessfully interviewed for the president's job were now offered positions as instructors. Marc Estrin, one of those instructors, told me that he considered Gerry "one of the most radical people I had ever met, with a far-reaching vision for Goddard College." Anyone with an exciting idea got an open-minded hearing from Gerry.

The timing seemed good for Walter's proposal to hire me. But the approval process dragged on from May through August without a decision. The reputation of the college as a freewheeling institution was such that my Goddard friends urged me to "just come up and talk your way in." However, when I returned at the end of August, I learned that a palace coup of sorts had taken place over the summer. A new body, the Educational Council, had been created to take the hiring process away from Gerry. Administrators, faculty, and students constituted this council, and they had legitimate fears that Gerry's laissez-faire hiring practices might eventually bankrupt the college. By the time of my arrival, they were closely vetting all new positions and proposals.

In mid-September, the word came down: no go for the position as Walter's assistant. By then my brother Jon had joined me in Vermont and we embarked (with my parents' aid) on the gutting and renovation of the 1820s house known as "the old Orr place," a former turkey farm. It was two miles from the spot where five dirt roads converged in the hamlet of Adamant, one of the five "post office villages" in the town of Calais. The village's name (as well as the adjective *adamant*) derived

There was no one quite like music instructor Dennis Murphy.

from the unyielding quality of the granite that had been mined years before in quarries just outside town.[13]

Some acquaintances of mine from those days still assume that, like them, I am a Goddard graduate. Why, they even saw me taking classes there. It's true: the Goddard instructors I met at the time didn't care who was enrolled and who wasn't. They longed for eager learners, regardless of their status at the school, who could get up in the morning and take part in the discussion. I took three classes during my first two years in Vermont that ranked with the best I had taken during my years at Columbia and UC Berkeley: Virginia Heffron's course Myth and Symbol, Marc Estrin's listening class in the Beethoven late quartets, and the Javanese gamelan ensemble, led by Dennis Murphy, who is to this date the only authentic mad genius I have ever encountered.

---

[13]The town was originally called Sodom—the biblical epitome of wickedness—by outsiders because, as the legend goes, the townspeople, mainly quarrymen, were too drunk to care whether their town had a name. In his book *Forever Calais*, local historian Weston Cate Jr. quotes a report in a *Montpelier Evening Argus* of 1905 that "efforts are being made to have the name changed to one more euphorious and with a better signification."

The Goddard campus, with its full enrollment at that time, was a lively place, and I spent many hours there. There were concerts by Mose Allison and Elvin Jones, readings by Allen Ginsberg and Anaïs Nin, and plays by David Mamet. (A recent Goddard graduate, Mamet had returned as a drama instructor.)

There were also films each Sunday night at the Haybarn Theater, but this was a haphazard affair, with student projectionists either showing up in an impaired state or forgetting to show up altogether. The Sunday night movies were a particular concern of a new friend, Ann Dumaresq Ryder, the coordinator of campus activities. Ann knew a lot about music, especially jazz, but not as much about film. She asked me to help her curate the Sunday night films. I wish I could remember that lineup for the fall of 1971, but there is a good chance that the list included films I had seen during the past five years at Columbia and Berkeley.

The only film I remember with certainty was Elia Kazan's *East of Eden*, which I had seen for the first time in Berkeley. Kazan's masterful direction and James Dean's heartbreaking performance affected me deeply then as now. My unofficial position as curator of the Sunday series gave me my first opportunity to share my own enthusiasms with many other moviegoers in a single evening. But I recall wondering as *East of Eden* unspooled if its long-ago setting (Salinas, California, in 1915) and its heart-on-the-sleeve emotionality made it a wise choice for (I'm guessing) a predominantly stoned audience.

Julie Harris and James Dean in *East of Eden*.

During those first two years as a transplant, I also met others outside of Goddard who were urban refugees like myself, whether from New York City, Philadelphia, or Boston. We found ourselves discussing what we loved about our new environment, but there was a common complaint: "I can't go to the movies any night I want to!" The first step in changing that situation was about to happen. The catalyst was a gift from a friend, a copy of Alexander Walker's book *Stanley Kubrick Directs*.

CHAPTER 8

A FILM SOCIETY IS BORN

A s I paged through Alexander Walker's book on Stanley Kubrick, I thought, "*The Killing...Lolita...Paths of Glory...Dr. Strangelove...* I'd love to see those films again." The book was a gift from my friend Joanne Risbano. A few years back, I had persuaded her to come with me to see *2001: A Space Odyssey*—my fourth time, her first. She was as impressed as I hoped she'd be and she guessed that I'd enjoy the book, especially after I told her about Leon's very tangential brush with Kubrick.

My daydream about seeing Kubrick's films evaporated quickly as I asked myself, "And what are the chances of seeing them around here?" Before I had a chance to give in to despair, I had a further thought: "The only way I'd see any of those films would be if I took the initiative to make it happen."[14]

For me, this was a radical idea. I had always been content to let others curate my film experiences; it never occurred to me to ask about getting involved in the film societies, first at Columbia and then at UC Berkeley. In retrospect, it seems I had a stunning lack of curiosity and imagination. These films did not appear by magic. There were students in my own class who selected the films and made it all happen. Now, living in rural

------

[14]One of my longtime Vermont friends, the late Larry Gordon, went through a similar evolution. Upon landing in central Vermont, he missed the choral music activity of Boston, so he founded the Word of Mouth Chorus and then Village Harmony in Plainfield.

The Pavilion Auditorium, home to the Lightning Ridge Film Society.

Vermont, the lack of opportunities to see classic or foreign films finally provided the impetus for me to take that fateful step from passive viewer to active participant, whatever form that might take.

I was seized by the possibility of a film society—like the ones that had expanded my vision in college—here in central Vermont. It may have been the very next day that I drove to nearby Montpelier, the state capital. The office of the recently established Vermont Council on the Arts on State Street seemed a good place to start. Perhaps it was a slow day, but I was directed immediately to the office of the agency's program director, Ellen McCullough Lovell.

Ellen turned out to be a guardian angel for the film society that was born then and there. I spilled out my inchoate idea and her immediate response was "Sure, we can do that." Next she said, "First, you need a place, and I think the Pavilion Auditorium would be ideal. Then you need a state sponsor in order to use it, and that would be us." I had been to the auditorium once and agreed; it had two hundred seats and a sloped floor. Until Ellen's suggestion, I hadn't given much thought to holding my screenings in Montpelier. Plainfield, with its thriving Goddard

College community in the early 1970s, was the center for most artistic and cultural activity in the region, and it had been the center of my own world thus far. Montpelier, by contrast, was the commercial and political center—in the parlance of 1972, "the straight world." But the prospect of a sloped floor and fixed seating was tantalizing.

The Pavilion Auditorium was located in the basement of the State Office Building and even had, on paper anyway, a projection room. In reality, this was an empty room with a projectionist's window ten feet up. The story I heard was that there was ultimately not enough money in the budget to properly outfit the room. I would have to be content with setting up a table in the back of the auditorium for two sixteen-millimeter projectors. Why two? So the audience would not have to wait for a reel change, which could take up to five minutes depending on the projectionist's dexterity. The location in the rear of the auditorium was not ideal—no audience member would want to sit in the back row near the whirring projectors—but it had to be good enough. And how would I get those projectors? Ellen suggested that I check the audio-visual department at the nearby Vermont State Library; surely I could borrow two from there. I already knew that film catalogs for ordering titles were on hand at Goddard, through Walter Ungerer; these would do, until I could order my own.

The one time I had been to the Pavilion Auditorium was for a showing of D.W. Griffith's 1920 silent classic *Way Down East*, shot mainly in White River Junction, Vermont. Knowledgeable friends told me that I should not miss an opportunity to hear Hazel Carlson of Morrisville provide the piano accompaniment. They were right—Hazel kept an eye on the screen while she used what sounded like eight hands on the piano. I didn't realize that the event was a benefit for Planned Parenthood of Vermont; it had been a deliberate choice to show a film whose central character is a young woman (Lillian Gish) who has been "done wrong" by a lover and is raising her child alone.

I also saw right away that this was a special evening in Montpelier; the audience was not the casually dressed crowd I was used to in Plainfield. It was my introduction to the capital city's "intelligentsia," many of whom I would soon get to know as regulars at the film society.

The showing of *Way Down East* was my first time in the Pavilion Auditorium.

More than twenty-five years later, I got a surprising insight into the world of early 1970s Montpelier that I had stepped into. One day I ran into my friend Jean Cate on the street. Jean had been an administrator at the Vermont Historical Society, housed on the ground floor of the Pavilion building. Every Friday at about 4 p.m. I'd get the key from Jean to unlock the door of the auditorium and haul my two borrowed projectors down there. Now, in the late 1990s, Jean stopped me on the street and said, "Rick, I have a confession to make. Remember all those years ago when you got the key from me?" Of course I did. "Well," Jean said, "I came so close to saying to you, 'What are you wasting your energy for? This town is so stuck in its ways it will never support anything like what you're doing.'" Jean continued, "I almost said it, but I bit my tongue. I saw how young and idealistic you were and I just couldn't burst your balloon." We shared a laugh. How glad we both were that she had been proved wrong.

The Montpelier that Jean described was changing rapidly in the early 1970s. As the late Yvonne Daley wrote in her book *Going Up the Country*, "The newcomers and the locals who joined them transformed the once-solidly conservative state into one of the nation's most progressive." One Goddard graduate, Ginny Callan, started a natural foods restaurant, Horn of the Moon Café; another, Fred Wilber, started the record store Buch Spieler. Visionary educators created Community College of Vermont, a radical rethinking of the college model. The Plainfield Food Co-op, twenty minutes from Montpelier, was one of many food cooperatives that would become an institution.

Political changes were also reconfiguring Vermont. In 1974, Patrick Leahy became the first Vermont Democrat ever to be elected to the U.S. Senate. And although Vermont had a reputation as a solidly conservative state, some elected Republicans took surprising stands. Our Republican senator, George Aiken, was an outspoken opponent of the Vietnam War ("Say we won and get out!" he urged), and our pro-business Republican governor, Deane Davis, inspired the creation of Act 250, which reined in the uncontrolled development that was threatening to despoil Vermont. A political outlier, recent arrival Bernie Sanders, ran unsuccessfully for the U.S. Senate in 1972 and for governor in 1974.[15] The time was riper than I knew for the start of the Lightning Ridge Film Society.

The name came from the road where I lived then and still do today.[16] A press release went to the Barre-Montpelier *Times Argus* and the Plainfield *Country Journal*. Leon, who was a master calligrapher, helped me design our flyer. Many of my movie-deprived friends eagerly awaited the first series. But was my intuition correct, that there was a larger audience out there?

I don't think I knew at the time what the phrase "film culture" meant, but as I go back to look at the offerings of the first Lightning Ridge season, I see that "film culture" perfectly described what I was doing. I had certainly been a participant in that phenomenon during

---

[15]Bernie would take Vermont's political evolution to the national stage starting with his shocking win (by ten votes!) in 1981 as Burlington's mayor. He was reelected three times and transformed Burlington, turning the neglected waterfront into one of the key attractions of the city. He was elected Vermont's sole representative to the U.S. Congress in 1991, serving until 2007, when he became one of our two senators. Quite a ride!

[16]When it came time years later to mandate addresses with road names for the new emergency 911 phone system, that road name spurred controversy in town. Was it "Lightning" (derived from the meteorological occurrence) or "Lightening" (derived from the practice of lightening wagonloads for the steep hill)? The latter position won out, but by that time the film society was no longer operating.

the 1960s, if one defines it as a passionate interest in films as both an art form and as a means of appreciating the life of our own society and that of earlier times.

My fellow film buffs and I—both my college friends of the late 1960s and my new acquaintances in Vermont—were excited by new films, but we were also eager to learn about their context. We had strong opinions about what we saw and were ready to engage with others who had a different take. Our attitude reflected the excitement that French and

Foreign Correspondent was on the first season's program.

Russian filmmakers displayed during the early days of "motion pictures": here was an art form that combined aspects of painting, theater, and literature into something totally new. As Bruce Kawin writes in *How Movies Work*: "Cinema itself is a coherent body of work and a manner of expression that has a history and a tradition and that builds on what has been learned and achieved in previous films. . . . To want to learn more about this is to be interested in film history."

Between the catalogs for United Artists, Films Incorporated, Universal Pictures, and others, I was able to program an ideal lineup. In the early 1970s, there was an entire distribution network known by its shorthand phrase "non-theatrical," covering film societies, schools, hospitals, and other institutions. Usually any film released earlier than two years previously was readily available, and not expensive.

LIGHTNING RIDGE *Film Society*

FRIDAY EVENINGS AT 8:30 P.M.
IN THE PAVILION AUDITORIUM IN MONTPELIER

MARCH 16 Dead of Night
A 1945 British supernatural thriller starring Michael Redgrave. "A variation of the Chinese Box Mystery, with enough testimony to the depths of human experience to give it top rank among the screen's thousands of melodramas." (Classics of the Foreign Film)

MARCH 23 East of Eden
James Dean's first and most electrifying screen performance highlights this modern version of the Cain and Abel story. Elia Kazan directed the adaptation of the John Steinbeck novel, set in Monterey, California in 1917.

MARCH 30 The Wrong Box
Based loosely on a Robert Louis Stevenson novel, this outlandish farce concerns a trust fund lottery in which the last surviving member falls heir to a sizeable fortune. Excellent comic performances by John Mills, Michael Caine, and Peter Sellers.

APRIL 6 Foreign Correspondent
Thrilling Alfred Hitchcock spy-chase in the tradition of "39 Steps" and "North by Northwest." Intrigue, suspense, and dark humor. Starring Joel McCrea and Laraine Day. 1940.

APRIL 13 What's Up, Tiger-Lily?
Woody Allen bought the rights to this Grade Z Japanese imitation of a James Bond thriller, and then re-dubbed it. The new plot revolves around agent Phil Moskowitz and a sought-after recipe for egg salad.

APRIL 20 The Killing
Sterling Hayden masterminds a racetrack robbery in Stanley Kubrick's first major film (1956). Kubrick utilized an ingenious narrative style and a sturdy cast to produce perhaps the most suspenseful and original "hold-up" film to date.

APRIL 27 Million Dollar Legs
W. C. Fields is the Prime Minister of Klopstokia ("a far away country") and Jack Oakie is the visiting brush salesman who organizes the Klopstokian Olympic team. American surrealist humor at its earliest and best (1933).

MAY 4 The Incredible Shrinking Man
A harrowing interpretation of Richard Matheson's science-fiction classic. Our hero gradually becomes smaller and smaller until . . . . A unique blend of fantasy, pathos, and metaphysics.

MAY 11 His Girl Friday
Cary Grant and Rosalind Russell star in Howard Hawks' classic comedy (1940). "A line is never allowed to reverberate but is quickly attached to another, funnier line . . . Still better than a clever, arch, extremely funny newspaper film." (Manny Farber)

MAY 18 Hunchback of Notre Dame
The spectacular silent version, featuring one of Lon Chaney's most famous characterizations.

MAY 25 Our Man in Havana
Carol Reed directed and Graham Greene wrote this subtle satire on British undercover activity in pre-Castro Cuba. It stars Alec Guinness as the vacuum cleaner salesman turned spy, and also features Burl Ives, Noel Coward, and Ernie Kovacs.

JUNE 1 Sullivan's Travels
Preston Sturges' incisive comedy of 1941 has been "the original '8½'". Joel McCrea portrays a film director tired of making trivia who sets out to bum around the country gathering material for a "meaningful" project.

JUNE 8 Mickey One
Many consider this atmospheric, almost "European" film to be Arthur Penn's finest. Warren Beatty is brilliant as a nightclub comic fleeing from unidentified gangsters.

JUNE 15 The Last Will of Dr. Mabuse
Fritz Lang fled Germany in 1932 after the Nazis confiscated this rarely-seen masterpiece. An amazing work on many levels, as political statement, as thrilling detective story, and as one of the most visually exciting films ever made.

JUNE 22 One-Eyed Jacks
"Marlon Brando's Western hero is closer to Heathcliff than to Hopalong Cassidy," says Andrew Sarris. This powerful version of the revenge myth, Brando's only directorial effort, is a highly individualized, intense, and haunting film.

Our very first program, 1973, with calligraphy by my father, Leon.

Out of the fifteen films on the schedule that first season, seven dated from the heyday of the Hollywood studio system, including *Million Dollar Movie* standards like *The Hunchback of Notre Dame, Foreign Correspondent, His Girl Friday,* and my old favorite *Million Dollar Legs.*

Some were more recent films I had seen in college (like *East of Eden*). There were British comedies (*Our Man in Havana* and *The Wrong Box*) and one subtitled film, Lang's *The Testament of Dr. Mabuse*, which had impressed me so much in Berkeley. As audiences eagerly awaited Stanley Kubrick's latest, *Barry Lyndon*, Lightning Ridge provided an opportunity to see his early thriller, *The Killing*. Arthur Penn's arty 1965 film *Mickey One* was a perfect example of how foreign films from that era influenced some of the more audacious Hollywood directors. *One-Eyed Jacks*, a 1961 film directed by and starring Marlon Brando, was an ambitious western with plenty of action and drama.

Lightning Ridge's debut film, on Friday, March 10, 1973, was one I had seen first in Berkeley and was eager to share with an unsuspecting audience: the 1945 British supernatural thriller *Dead of Night*. Although the chances were good that few people had heard of the film, the auditorium was full and I had an immediate answer about attracting a wider net of filmgoers. The only bad moment that night was when the Pavilion custodian, a lovely man named Eddie DuBois, thought he was being helpful by turning the lights up when the end credits appeared. He didn't know (because I had forgotten to tell him) that the film's final twist plays out as those credits unroll.

•

Lightning Ridge also provided me with an opportunity to broaden my own film education. One example: After showing *Sullivan's Travels*, I became interested in the films that Preston Sturges wrote before he became one of Hollywood's first writer/directors. Some of these films were directed by Mitchell Leisen, and one in particular, the poignant comedy-drama *Remember the Night*, with Barbara Stanwyck and Fred MacMurray, was featured at Lightning Ridge. I started to hunt down other Leisen films and saw Billy Wilder's name on some of the writing credits. Even though I appreciated *Midnight* (written by Wilder) and *Easy Living* (written by Sturges), I learned that both Sturges and Wilder thought that Leisen had ruined their scripts, fueling their determination to write AND direct their own films.

My curiosity about Wilder's own screenwriting career led me to the films of Ernst Lubitsch (Lubitsch's comedy *Ninotchka*, starring Greta

Garbo, was co-written by Wilder). This in turn opened up a subject that fascinates me to this day, the complex story of the Eastern European Jewish emigrés in Hollywood. I realized that there was a direct line between the German Expressionism of the 1920s, the rise of Nazism, the emigration of Jews, and the birth of film noir. Many of the directors, like Fritz Lang, Robert Siodmak, Otto Preminger, and Billy Wilder, were Austrian or German exiles who came of artistic age during the prime years of what has come to be known as German Expressionism, in which the focus was on representing emotional states rather than depicting reality. The directors brought Expressionism's charged atmosphere, deep shadows, and unusual angles to the films they made after landing in Hollywood in the 1930s and 1940s.

The more I've learned about what is involved in making and distributing a film (mainly inflated egos, compromises, and large-scale financial anxiety), the more I'm convinced that the exhibition end of the chain may be the most gratifying. It's only here that one can regularly meet the audience as they leave the theater and hear their heartfelt thank-you's. I got my first taste of this satisfaction in those early days of the Lightning Ridge film series—and learned at the same time that there were other draws for audience members besides the films themselves. Kathy Gips remembered Friday nights as a social occasion as well; because there was only one show on one night, she said, "you knew your friends would be there." The films were the main attraction, said Ellen David-Friedman, "but for those of us living in drafty houses, there was also the pleasure of a warm auditorium for a few hours."

Steve Bissette was a high school student with a newly acquired driver's license, who regularly attended with one or two friends. "There weren't many films we missed. There was a remarkable access to films going back to the silent era," Steve told me. "We really counted on you. It was as if I ordered helpings of film history on some sort of menu." At the same time, Steve and his friends were also sampling the offerings of film societies at the University of Vermont and in Waitsfield, a half-hour south of Montpelier. Lightning Ridge stood out for the comfortable seats and the quality of the sound. For the latter, I had   the Kodak Pageant projectors borrowed from the State

Library to thank; a knob on the side of those machines improved the clarity of the sound track.

Two other teenagers I got to know were brought by their parents to many Friday night films. Anne LaBrusciano remembered that her parents probably never checked the appropriateness of any given film. "I might have been eleven or twelve," Anne recalled, "when my parents took me to see *The Exterminating Angel*." That dark and disturbing 1962 film, by Luis Buñuel, is set at a dinner party in a wealthy Mexico City neighborhood. The guests are seized by a mysterious inability to leave the room. As they are trapped there day after day, the story becomes a drawing-room version of *Lord of the Flies*. "I didn't know what I was seeing, but I've never forgotten it," Anne said. A decade later, Anne became our first video clerk at Downstairs Video. She stayed with us for about twenty years, not only at the video counter but operating the projectors, scooping popcorn, and curating our Children's Film Series.

Tom Blachly was another teenager who accompanied his parents to many screenings. "This was a very formative experience for me as a teen living in Vermont in the '70s," he remembered. "Back then there were no other opportunities to see classic films, so watching them was a complete revelation to me, and led to a lifetime appreciation of film." It was a particular satisfaction that many years later, Tom and I collaborated for five years on curating a monthly film series for the Jaquith Library in nearby Marshfield.

Another person who rarely missed a film was Andrea Serota, who first came to the Film Society's showings after a few years of living in rural Maine. When she saw the schedule of films, she said, "I thought I had died and gone to heaven." She recalled noticing me for the first time on a Friday night in 1977 that was memorable for me for other reasons. I was the projectionist that night, showing one of my childhood favorites, *Tight Little Island* (a.k.a. *Whisky Galore*). I noticed five minutes before the end that the film had jumped its track and was not being wound by the take-up reel. I had to make a split-second decision: do I stop the film just minutes before the end and fix it (I could hear the groans), or do I tear the film in two, let it run onto the floor, and deal with the mess afterward? I chose the latter, even knowing that five minutes equals a lot of film. By the time Andrea was walking up the aisle, she saw me knee-deep in celluloid, trying to figure out where to start reconstituting the film. Two months later we met, and we were married in 1983.

The Lightning Ridge Film Society lasted eight years and by my rough estimate showed about 250 films. We hosted not only the two seasons per year of Friday night films, but also other ancillary series. When I sensed that the appetite for newer foreign films was growing, I began our Contemporary World Cinema series, featuring films recently released on 16-millimeter, such as Federico Fellini's *The Clowns* and Luis Buñuel's *The Discreet Charm of the Bourgeoisie*, at Montpelier's Union Elementary School auditorium.

I also enjoyed a rewarding relationship with the recently established Community College of Vermont (CCV). Under the leadership of Peter Smith, Don Hooper, and Margery Walker, CCV was eager to form partnerships with community organizations. For a few years, it co-sponsored with Lightning Ridge a Monday night classic film series at Montpelier's Christ Church.

My relationship with CCV extended to teaching a film appreciation course for two semesters, my first experience in both designing a curriculum and leading a class. On one occasion, I had a pedagogic brainstorm. The print (i.e., the sixteen-millimeter copy of the film) for the scheduled Lightning Ridge showing of Robert Altman's unusual gangster drama *Thieves Like Us* arrived early enough to show in class. After the film, I handed out a rave review of the film by Pauline Kael in the *New Yorker* and a pan by Gary Arnold in the *Washington Post*. The assignment was to read each, then go back a few nights later to see the film again at the public screening. We had a lively discussion the following week about whether the students' initial reactions to the film were changed as a result of reading the reviews.

The success of Lightning Ridge was such that by 1978, I added an extra show on Friday nights. Instead of one screening at 7 p.m., there were now two, at 6:30 and 9 (strange to think of now, when a 10 p.m. bedtime constitutes a late night). This is where things stood in the spring of 1980, when I got the chance to take the giant leap from a film society to a seven-nights-a-week cinema.

▣ TRAILER:
SULLIVAN'S TRAVELS

Duringthe first season of the Lightning Ridge Film Society, I took special delight in sharing a film I had discovered only the year before while watching late-night television. My new home in Adamant had no television antenna, so there was no reception for either the CBS affiliate in Burlington or the NBC affiliate in Plattsburgh, New York. But the signal of Channel 8, the ABC affiliate in Poland Spring, Maine, was beamed from the top of Mount Washington in New Hampshire. From those heights, it reached Adamant with no interference.

Like many of the New York City channels from my youth, Channel 8 (technically WMTW-TV) had both a late-night schedule to fill and access to old Hollywood movies. It wasn't *Million Dollar Movie*, but it was something. One night I came home from Plainfield just in time for the start of Preston Sturges' inside-Hollywood comedy *Sullivan's Travels*,

Joel McCrea and Veronica Lake in Preston Sturges' *Sullivan's Travels*.

from 1941. The title was vaguely familiar to me. *US Camera*, an annual photography book that my parents bought each year, featured a production still in the 1942 edition. But that was all I knew. Preston Sturges was an unfamiliar name to me, unlike his contemporaries John Huston, Billy Wilder, and John Ford.

That night I was dazzled by the wit, the headlong pace, and the general high spirits of the film, which starred Joel McCrea and Veronica Lake. McCrea, as John Sullivan, is a successful director of comedies who wants to make a serious film about the ills of the world. The name of that film-within-a-film: *O Brother, Where Art Thou?* In 2000, filmmakers Joel and Ethan Coen paid homage to Sturges by making a Depression-set film of that name, a film the fictional Sullivan might have made.

After that introduction to Sturges in 1971, I learned that Sturges had written and directed seven hit comedies in a row from 1940 to 1945. Unfortunately, all it took was a few consecutive flops to render him all but unemployable. At the time of his death in 1958, his name was forgotten. But in the early 1970s, a collective unconscious was at work: just at the time a chance discovery led me to *Sullivan's Travels*, film societies and revival cinemas across the country were rediscovering the work of this brilliant man who lovingly satirized American culture. Starting in 1972, each new Lightning Ridge season featured a Sturges film (*The Lady Eve, The Palm Beach Story, The Miracle of Morgan's Creek, Hail the Conquering Hero*). The film society platform gave me a chance to catch up with the titles I hadn't seen. If the audience enjoyed them too, so much the better.

I learned a lesson about the importance of an audience when I screened one of the lesser-known Sturges comedies. I had never seen the 1948 film *Unfaithfully Yours*, but the Sturges name was enough for me. In that film, Rex Harrison is a famous orchestra conductor (modeled on Sir Thomas Beecham) who suspects his wife of infidelity. Strains of Rossini, Wagner, and Tchaikovsky accompany his three different fantasies about how he will deal with the situation.

A few days before the public showing, I ran the film at home to both check out the print and have a sneak preview. To me that night, the film was decidedly not funny and its peculiar tone was in poor taste. I feared facing a hostile audience that Friday night. But to my surprise and delight, what was a lead balloon to an audience of one was a "laff riot" (as the entertainment rag *Variety* might say) to a full house. I was now able to appreciate the dark humor in the film and was relieved when several people stopped me on the way out to thank me for giving them the opportunity to laugh so hard.

CHAPTER 9

"WHAT'S HAPPENING ON MAIN STREET?"

During our childhood and adolescence, my brother Jon and I had spent many hours in our father's Cross County Art Center in Yonkers, which was at that time the only art-supplies store and frame shop in Westchester County. When we both landed in Vermont in 1970, we were struck by the absence of such a store in Montpelier; the nearest one was on Church Street in Burlington, an hour away. In May 1975, Jon and his wife, Suzanne Rexford-Winston, opened the Drawing Board at 39 Barre Street. By 1978, the store had moved to 22 Main Street, where it has remained a popular fixture in downtown Montpelier. Jon's landlord at the Drawing Board was Ernest Massucco, whose family had lived in Montpelier for many years. Since the early part of the twentieth century, the building housing 22-24-26 Main Street was known as the Massucco Block. Ernest Massucco, now elderly, was eager to find a buyer for the building and offered it to Jon at a very fair price. The papers were signed in early 1980, and almost immediately Jon and I realized, with mounting excitement, that the building could house a permanent home for the Lightning Ridge Film Society.

In the early years of operating the film society, I hadn't thought about a theater as the end result. Once-a-week showings were enough for me. But after 1978, I noticed that the film society audiences had increased enough to warrant a second showing. Consequently, I had the growing intuition that the Central Vermont community would

Free Press Special Photo by DAVE GOSKA

NEW THEATER FOR CAPITAL CITY
. . . old Savoy being restored for film screenings

The first news of the Savoy Theater, July 1980.

support an art movie theater that would show the fare so popular with the Lightning Ridge audience. Establishing such a theater now seemed a logical, thrilling—and scary—next step. Jon now owned the Massucco Block and was as eager as I was to see a cinema there. The space then occupied by Emslie the Florist appeared to have the ideal contours— long and narrow—for an intimate theater. When would an opportunity like this come again?

Looking back, I recognize another reason for my blind optimism: everywhere I looked there were creative ventures that found an astonishing degree of community support. I have previously mentioned institutions such as Hunger Mountain Co-op and Community College of Vermont, and businesses such as Horn of the Moon Café, Bear Pond Books, and the record store Buch Spieler. There were also performance groups like the Two Penny Circus and the Bread and Puppet Theater, music ensembles like the Onion River Chorus and the Fyre and Lightning Consort, and feisty political organizations like the Liberty Union party. In Plainfield, Jules and Helen Rabin started the area's first artisanal bakery, Upland Bakers, while Joey Klein and Betsy Ziegler established the organic Littlewood Farm. New ideas in education led to the Center School and New School in Plainfield and the open classrooms of Union-32 High School in East Montpelier.

Then there was my own experience in establishing Lightning Ridge Concerts, which sponsored folk music events from 1974 through 1980. When I was growing up, I had been exposed to folk music of all kinds, and in the spirit of those times, I now thought that others in central Vermont might be interested as well. Thanks to the contacts of my brother Winnie (a banjo and pedal steel guitar player) and the proximity of Philo Records in North Ferrisburg, I was able to present musicians like Rosalie Sorrels, Jim Ringer, Mary McCaslin, and Jody Stecher.

I also presented traditional musicians from the British Isles who were on tour in America, at either the Unitarian Church in Montpelier or at the former Grange Hall in Plainfield. Our memorable guests included Alastair Anderson from Northumberland, England; Joe and Antoinette McKenna from Dublin, Ireland; and Artie Tresize and Cilla Fisher from Fife, Scotland.

In short, Central Vermont in 1980 was far from the cultural desert that my friend Jean Cate had bemoaned when she had painted a picture of Montpelier in the 1960s. If there ever was a time and place to begin an artistically and financially risky venture, it was here and now. So in the summer of 1980, Jon and I, putting aside our doubts, began to plan for a small, one-screen theater, aiming for a November opening.

•

What was the new theater to be called? We tossed around several ideas before, eventually, the solution came from an unexpected source, Ernest Massucco himself.

One day during the period of ownership transition, Mr. Massucco came into the Drawing Board. "So what are you boys intending to do with the building?" he asked. Jon explained that the space then occupied by the florist would probably become a movie theater. "Why, that's interesting," Mr. Massucco said. "I'm pretty sure that there used to be a theater in the Emslie space, back in the nickelodeon days . . . and it was called the Savoy." He further explained that his family had emigrated from the Savoia region of Italy. Jon and I looked at each other and no discussion was needed. Not only did the name exude class, but it would be an apt closing of a historic Montpelier circle.

Over the years, people have asked me how the Savoy got its name, and they have been surprised to hear it bore no relation to Richard D'Oyly Carte's Savoy Theatre, of Gilbert and Sullivan fame, in London. That venue—or should I say "theatre"?—inspired many Savoys in the English-speaking world as a name that denotes high-toned but popular entertainment. Lately, though, I've discovered that our Savoy here in Montpelier actually does bear some relation to Carte's London theater, which presented premieres of *H.M.S. Pinafore, The Pirates of Penzance*, and other favorites.

Richard D'Oyly Carte of Gilbert and Sullivan and the original Savoy Theater fame.

To understand this history, we have to go back to the eleventh century, when the authority of the state of Savoie stretched through much of the Alps, taking in parts of what are now both France and Italy. The etymology goes something like this: the name Sapaudia was a Latinization of the local words for "forest" or "upland forest." Over time, it evolved first into Saboia and then into the Italian Savoia. In France, the region was called Savoie, and in England, Savoy.

One member of the ruling House of Savoy was Eleanor of Provence, queen consort of the English king Henry III. Eleanor's uncle Peter (or

Piers, or Piero) of Savoy came with her to London. King Henry made Peter the Earl of Richmond and, in 1246, gave him land in central London, where Peter built the Savoy Palace in 1263. Upon Peter's death, the Savoy tract was given to Edmund, First Earl of Lancaster, by his mother, Queen Eleanor, and then passed to Edmund's great-granddaughter, Blanche.

In 1864 a fire burned everything except the stone walls and the Savoy Chapel. The property sat empty until Richard D'Oyly Carte bought it in 1880 to build the Savoy Theatre, specifically for the production of the Gilbert and Sullivan operas that he was producing. So in a convoluted way, our tiny theater in Montpelier and the famed one in London share some French-Italian ancestry, linked by the immigration of the Massucco family from that very region.

Shortly after word circulated that there would be a "new"

THE MASSUCCO
Moving
Picture

THEATRE

_____

WEDNESDAY AND THURSDAY.

From Darkness to Dawn.

A very pathetic picture, shows the lovers—the elopement—bad luck—the accident—Happy family reunion, all's well.

_____

The Tenor With the Leather Lungs.

For a side splitting film do not fail to see this. It has got them all guessing.

_____

SONG :
"Alice, Where Art Thou Going?"
Sung by Ernest Fisher,
A. L. Poole, Pianist.

_____

☞ This building is fire proof and has three exits and is equipped with fire extinguishers.

ADMISSION 5 CENTS.

S. Massucco, Manager.   26 Main St.
135tf

Before the Savoy, it was the Massucco Moving Picture Theater.

Savoy Theater on Main Street, we had a surprise visit from Eric Bardrof, proprietor of Country Camera, just down the block. He was rummaging in his store's basement and found a 1910 photo showing the marquee displaying a Savoy Theatre (with an "-re") sign. Soon someone else—it might have been Montpelier historian Perry Merrill—brought copies of ads from the _Montpelier Evening Argus_—movie announcements for the fare at 26 Main Street. The venue, I learned, was known as the Massucco Moving Picture Theatre from its inception in 1907 until it was renamed the Savoy Theatre in 1910.

Whenever I look at these ads, I'm curious about what the interior of the theater looked like and how the films were projected. I want to know about the content of those films (which are probably lost forever). Some titles are *The Tenor with the Leather Lungs, Mr. Bondage,* and *A Pair of Schemers,* whose plot was described in the ad: "An uncle decides to say who his nephew should marry, but the young man does as he pleases and marries his own choice. The uncle suddenly appears and interesting and lively complications follow." No plot is mentioned for the "very comical" film *How Rastus Got His Pork Chops,* but I shudder to think what that short film was about.[17]

The ads also tell us that the Savoy often presented musical interludes at these films. "E. Galaise" and "Miss Eva Richards" are the singers mentioned in several notices, as is their accompanying pianist, "Miss Ione Ghio." The song advertised in the *Argus* of August 20, 1908, was "I'll Be Waiting for You, Dearie, When You Come Home."

Turning a once-a-week film society into a seven-nights-a-week movie theater meant that there was much to be done. Clearly the administration of the Savoy could not be a one-person job, as the film society had been.[18] I starting searching for a person who might run the theater with me—someone who knew more about balancing a budget and paying bills than I did (a low bar), who enjoyed contact with the public, and who had a devotion to film. I didn't have to look further than the Goddard College bookstore.

Gary Ireland had been hired by Goddard in the mid-1970s with a mandate to make the bookstore functional after years of chaos. Gary and

---

[17] There were several films in the "Rastus" series, all released before the infamous *Birth of a Nation* appeared in 1915. As Henry Louis Gates Jr. writes in *Stony the Road,* "How many watermelons does a person have to devour, how many chickens does an individual have to steal, to make the point that black people are manifestly, by nature, both gluttons and thieves?"

[18] I did have some help during the Lightning Ridge Film Society years, so thanks are due to Beth Barndt, Louis Berney, Ellie Hayes, Dianne Kearns, Tony Klein, Andrew Kline, Suzanne Rexford-Winston, and Marc Rubenstein.

A photo from 1910 was discovered in the basement of Country Camera.

I had many conversations at the bookstore, and invariably they wound up on the subject of movies and the lack of variety in our area. Over some months, I learned about Gary's background: a native Kansan, he had gone to divinity school and become a minister in inner-city Detroit ("the token white minister" in a largely black congregation, Gary would say). The turmoil of the 1960s became an inner turmoil for him, as well. He left the ministry, eventually moving to Ann Arbor, Michigan, and managing a bookstore there until he came to Goddard in 1978.

One summer day in 1980, I ran into Gary at the summit of Owl's Head Mountain in the nearby Groton State Forest. As we gazed at the spectacular view of Kettle Pond, we shared a conversation about our plans. I hadn't known that Goddard was undergoing one of its periodic retrenchment periods and that Gary's future at the bookstore might not be secure. With my need for someone with practical business experience in mind, I asked him to consider leaving Goddard to join me in setting up the theater. When he responded with a "yes," he explained that he had had a bit of an epiphany on a weekend trip to Boston. He had been to a restaurant that had just opened, and the air was crackling

Gary Ireland and me in the Savoy lobby-to-be, December 1980.

with excitement. "It must be thrilling to be part of something new and different in a community that you knew well," he said. "I don't know that much about films, but there was a time I didn't know that much about books, either."

Gary did know enough about films to bring a discerning eye, though. He told me of his intense reaction on seeing his first-ever foreign film while in college, Ingmar Bergman's *The Virgin Spring*. Bergman's stark, violent revenge drama, set in the Middle Ages, was a universe apart from the films he had seen before, and it opened his eyes to the potential of film to do more than entertain. He became enthralled with the possibility of opening other people's eyes to film art.

Animal Crackers: a film that began a fruitful relationship.

•

And now: where to get seats, projectors, tickets, the inevitable popcorn machine? How were we going to establish relationships with distributors and how were we going to figure out which films to play? Here is where John Morrison, a crucial figure in our history, comes in. It might be said that I owe one of the Savoy Theater's most important and lasting personal relationships to the Marx Brothers.

For many years, the 1932 film *Animal Crackers*, which contains some of the brothers' zaniest skits, had been rarely shown. Paramount Pictures had relinquished the rights in 1950, and those rights reverted to the authors of the original stage play, Morrie Ryskind and George S. Kaufman. While I was a student at Columbia, I had gone to a rare screening at the long-since-demolished Huntington Hartford Museum, at New York's Columbus Circle. It was a special treat to hear Groucho sing "Hooray for Captain Spaulding" (the theme music for his much later long-running TV quiz show *You Bet Your Life*) and to hear him deliver the line, "One morning I shot an elephant in my pajamas. How he got into my pajamas I'll never know."

In the mid-1970s, *Animal Crackers* remained the only Marx Brothers movie not readily available for rental. My college friend Matt Weinstein was now attending grad school and was serving on the programming committee of the Amherst Film Cooperative in Northampton, Massachusetts. The Cooperative had come into possession of a rare 16-millimeter print. Was I interested? Of course! I drove to Northampton and the print was handed to me by the Cooperative's co-director, and that is how I met John Morrison, who was to play an important role in the life of the Savoy and later Downstairs Video.

John's film society eventually morphed into the Pleasant Street Theater in Northampton, owned by John and his business partner, Richard Pini. John and Richard were eager to show Gary and me the ins and outs of the business, the behind-the-scenes necessities for operating a full-time movie theater. They told us where to look for seats, a screen, and movie projectors. Gary and I—and sometimes my brother Jon—made at least four trips to Northampton to study the Pleasant Street systems. It was on one of those trips that John Morrison made a generous offer. He would book our films gratis for our first year, or until we felt confident to make those calls ourselves.

Beyond that material support, what John gave us was confidence that we could actually open our own theater, with its own character, in our own community. A great believer in film culture, he loved the idea that a town even smaller than Northampton would have its own art cinema.

•

Recently I came upon an artifact that I thought had long since disappeared: a three-inch piece of yellow card stock that I carried around with me during the summer and fall of 1980. In those days, I had trouble running a simple errand on Main or State Street without someone pressing me with questions about the rumored theater.

ANSWERS TO THE TEN MOST COMMONLY-
ASKED QUESTIONS ABOUT THE "SAVOY"

1 ~~Around Thanksgiving~~ Early December
2 "Casablanca," if possible
3 Seven nights a week
4 All kinds--new & old, U. S. &
   foreign
5 Yes, I am very excited
6 Yes, there will be popcorn
7 142 seats
8 Three dollars
9 No, we will not show "Rocky
   Horror Picture Show"
10 Maybe

The FAQ card I carried with me during the fall of 1980.

Long before the acronym FAQ entered our vocabulary, the heading of my typed card was "Answers to the Ten Most Frequently Asked Questions about the Savoy."

The answer to Number One was "Early December"; this was written in pencil, after the original "Around Thanksgiving" was crossed out. However, this, too, proved to be overly optimistic as October turned into November. Number Two was "*Casablanca*, if possible." This turned out to be true, but not in the way we had planned. Number Three was "Seven nights a week," an exciting prospect for Central Vermonters who had to wait from one Friday to the next to get their Lightning Ridge movie fix. Number Four was "All kinds: new and old, U.S. and foreign." And Number Five was "Yes, I am excited."

And, indeed, I was excited. The process of opening the Savoy was thrilling, though not without its share of angst. While Jon and his construction crew (David Van de Sande, Jim Donnon, and John McCullough) figured out how to build the sloped floor, the framing for the screen, the concession counter, and the projection booth,

What's Happening On Montpelier's Main Street?

MASSUCCO BLOCK RESTORATION

John Winston has exceptional plans for the restoration of The Massucco Block. Winston is proprietor of the Drawing Board and purchased the block a couple of years ago. The upstairs has eight apartments, all of which are occupied, and the building is being renovated with a taste and quality that can only add to Montpelier's downtown district.

The storefront adjacent to the Drawing Board was once Emslie's Florists, but in 1908 it was a nickelodeon where the price of an evening's entertainment was the small sum of five cents. Winston plans to return that section of the Massucco Block to theater, giving theatergoers a variety of well-planned entertainment. There will be two shows a night, with a blend of first-run movies, some foreign and some revival. Although the theater will be completely new and equipped with air conditioning, the decor will be kept as a period piece.

Construction is forthcoming in the near future with a hopeful opening in late

Four doors down from the Fir man building, brothers Rick a John Winston are renovating a st into a movie theater which w Montpelier's silent film theater fr 1908 to 1914.

Known then as the Sav Theatre, it will carry that na again when it opens, probably mid-October.

Rick Winston, who has been in charge of a local film society sin 1973, said he "had been looking space for quite some time" to est lish a permanent theater.

Winston said the 150-seat thea "will try to retain something of c original space. But there are known early photographs of it."

The Savoy, which housed ma retail shops over the years, w have a two-foot rise built from fr

Times Argus headline heralding the construction of the Savoy, fall 1980.

Gary and I were figuring out the logistics of the day-to-day running of the operation. I'm sure John Morrison regularly received a "What do we do now?" call.

John had given us leads for purveyors of seats and screen, projection and concession equipment. We traveled to Boston to pick up a used popcorn machine, one that still had the instructions on it for how to add Red Dye #40. This, we learned, was the secret ingredient in giving movie-theater popcorn the irresistible-to-some yellow glow. That was one of our first easy decisions: no yellow glow.

On one freezing day, a truck arrived carrying our 140 seats. We formed a bucket brigade of sorts, passing the seats from one to another up to the second floor for storage, since the theater floor had not been completed. The same used-theater-equipment-person helped us install the screen which, to our surprise, was a glossy rubber sheet with small perforations (creating the perceived depth of the projected image).

The installation of the projectors had to wait until the booth was finished. Our two projectionists-to-be, Andrew Kline and Norman Bloom, studied the best they could without an actual machine on hand. The two machines that finally arrived actually weren't projectors at all, but parts from six different projectors, which were then reconstituted before our eyes by a wizard from Boston, Norm Miller.

One big difference between handling 35-millimeter film at the Savoy as opposed to the 16-millimeter films at the Pavilion was the necessity for splicing. The films I showed at the Pavilion came on three reels. I'd set up reel two on the second projector as the first reel neared its end and then set up reel three where reel one had been. In the "grown-up" world of professional projection, the films came in two octagonal metal cans containing three reels each. (The cans are known in the industry as "Goldbergs" since the Goldberg Brothers of Denver, Colorado, cornered the market early in the history of the industry.) Three reels of film from the first can would be spliced together on a special table to make one big reel, shown on the first projector, while the second three would be spliced for use on the second projector.

The eponymous "Goldbergs" were made by the Goldberg Brothers of Denver.

We had a plan for the days before our opening. Norman and Andrew would put our first feature, *Casablanca*, together, project it, take it apart, splice it back together, project it, etc., getting the hang of the splicing table and projectors. It was a good idea in theory, but after going to the bus station to collect our "Goldberg" cans, we discovered that the first can contained reels one to three of *Casablanca* while the second can contained the first three reels of Bob Fosse's film *Lenny*, with Dustin Hoffman starring as the controversial comic Lenny Bruce. There was a frantic call to United Artists in Boston ("This never happens, believe me!" their salesperson said), and a promise that the missing *Casablanca* can would arrive the next day—coincidentally, the day of our opening.

That opening wasn't "around Thanksgiving," as I had written on my FAQ card. It wasn't "early December," either. Originally, the Australian

We tried, but failed, to open on schedule.

Finally — opening!

film *My Brilliant Career* had been scheduled to be our first film, starting on January 2, with *Casablanca* to follow. Around mid-December, though, we had reluctantly concluded that the opening day of January 2 was not realistic, either—too much painting and other detail work yet to do—and therefore *My Brilliant Career* was bumped until later in the winter.[19] So it was that *Casablanca*, by default, did turn out to be our opening film—and the film that we subsequently showed for free on each important Savoy anniversary.

In the meantime, there were important details to execute. Linda Mirabile and Mason Singer, of Laughing Bear Associates, designed our stationery and logo. Phil Godenschwager at Great American Salvage took on the daunting task of constructing an eye-catching marquee. It was Phil's first attempt at an electrical sign, and as he recently confessed to me, his last. The marquee that he installed—with a few days to spare—was spectacular, but it wasn't long before the extremes of winter and summer played havoc with the approximately two hundred bulbs.

There was one event that nearly derailed our opening: the final inspection by the Department of Labor and Industry. Our aisle, the

---

[19] I thought of Jacques Tati, who had directed a brilliant film in 1967, *Playtime,* whose forty-minute centerpiece takes place in a chic restaurant that has opened a week too early. I foresaw similar chaos engulfing us, if on a smaller scale.

inspector said, was two inches too narrow. Jon had measured stanchion to stanchion across the aisle, but the inspector measured from armrest to armrest. We tried to go through the chain of command for a waiver, but no one wanted to take responsibility for that decision. Finally, we reached Joel Cherington, the commissioner of the Labor and Industry Department, and he agreed to take a look. After a very tense walk-through, he said, "Seems OK to me, but how about putting in another exit sign at the front?"

With that, we were ready to fire up the popcorn machine, turn on the marquee, and start inviting an eager crowd in to watch *Casablanca*. It was Friday, January 9, 1981.

THE TIMES ARGUS, BARRE-MONTPELIER, VT. SATURDAY, JANUARY 10, 1981

Montpelier's Savoy Theatre looked suitably misty Friday night as the new cinema opened its doors to a packed house for the classic *Casablanca*. Owner Rick Winston said the 8 pm. show was sold out and people had to be turned away at the door. (Pirie photo)

After a sold-out opening night.

2006 Green Mountain Film Festival cover art by Mary Azarian.

PART 3

"AND...ACTION!!"
1981-1999

CHAPTER 10

BUMPS IN THE ROAD

It didn't take long for reality to set in after our popular opening week of *Casablanca*. Our next two films—Werner Herzog's 1972 film *Aguirre, the Wrath of God* and Robert Altman's 1971 *McCabe and Mrs. Miller*—drew small audiences. Things improved somewhat with the Spencer Tracy–Katharine Hepburn comedy *Pat and Mike*. The programs for that first winter proceeded as we had planned, with a mix of American and foreign films, old and newer ones. I say "newer" rather than "new" because we didn't have the legitimacy yet to deal with major distributors who released the current films.

We learned quickly that the well-established Capitol Theater, a few blocks away on State Street (which was to add a second screen that summer), already had accounts and long-standing relationships with Columbia, Paramount, Universal, and Warner Brothers; it was a matter of course that it would be showing the studio fare. But a film we showed that April of 1981 gave us some ideas for maneuvering around this obstacle. It was a drama called *Resurrection*, which starred Ellen Burstyn as a woman who discovers she has unexplained healing powers after a near-fatal auto accident. It had been released in early 1980 by Universal Pictures, but deemed to be a commercial failure. Therefore, it was ours if we wanted it. In this way, we showed Jonathan Demme's *Melvin and Howard*, also distributed by Universal, later that spring.

THE SAVOY THEATER

26 Main Street/Montpelier/Vermont 05602 (802)229-0509

My Brilliant Career

Saturday Jan. 3-Tuesday Jan. 6

One of last year's most popular and well-received films was, according to the Vanguard Press, "a gorgeously filmed, witty Australian film about a young woman from a poor farm family who fights to pursue an independent career in the arts. The Victorian Age she happens to be living in would rather have her married off. Judy Davis (the resemblance to the young Katherine Hepburn is striking) stars as Sybylla Melvyn and Gill Armstrong provides the fluid, emotion-laden direction".

Sat. 5:30, 8, 10:30; Sun. 4, 6:30, 9; Mon.-Tues. 6:30, 9

Casablanca

Wednesday Jan. 7-Tuesday Jan. 13

The strange allure of the story of the expatriate cafe owner (Humphrey Bogart) and the woman he once loved (Ingrid Bergman) has never been completely explained; Andrew Sarris referred to it as the prime example of the "Happy Accident school of film-making". Whether functioning as a political allegory, popular myth, psychological analysis, or romantic melodrama, "Casablanca" remains perhaps the most popular American film to date. The outstanding supporting cast includes Peter Lorre, Sydney Greenstreet, Paul Henreid, and Conrad Veidt. (1942)

Mon.-Thu. 6:30, 8:45; Fri.-Sat. 5:30, 8, 10:30; Sun. 4, 6:30, 8:45

McCabe & Mrs. Miller

Wednesday Jan. 14-Tuesday Jan. 20

In Robert Altmans compelling re-creation of the American frontier, Warren Beatty is McCabe, the grizzled, small-time gambler whose business is bringing pleasure to the zinc-mining town of Presbyterian Church; Julie Christie is   nosed madam who coerces him int
          'ms

Pat and Mike

Wednesday Jan. 28-Tuesday Feb. 3

The Boston Phoenix: " 'Pat and Mike' gets our vote for the best of the Katherine Hepburn-Spencer Tracy films—as well as for the best screen-writing effort by Garson Kanin and Ruth Gordon. Hepburn plays a talented golf pro unappreciated by her stolid boy friend, and Tracy is the somewhat seedy sports promoter who manages her. Love ensues, naturally, but it's almost unphysical, more a joyous mutual admiration. The film is uproariously funny, gracefully directed by George Cukor, and full of pungent supporting performances". (1952)

Mon.-Thu. 6:30, 9; Fri.-Sat. 5:30, 8, 10:00; Sun. 4, 6:30, 9

Get Out your Handkerchiefs

Wednesday Feb. 4-Tuesday Feb. 10

One of the most popular foreign films in years and for good reason! "Handkerchiefs" is a daring comedy that challenges sexual myths and attitudes. Gerard Depardieu is the young husband whose wife (Carole Laure) has fallen into an alarming depression; he enlists the assistance of a Mozart-fixated stranger (Patrick Dewaere) in an attempt to snap her out of it. The two men become great buddies dedicated to keeping her happy once she finds the answer to her depressed state; a misunderstood 13 year old boy with a 200 I.Q. Bertrand Blier's film is "flagrantly funny", says Pauline Kael, "a film that makes you unreasonably happy".

Mon.-Thu. 6:30, 9; Fri.-Sat. 5:30, 8, 10:30; Sun. 4, 6:30, 9

Dr. Strangelove

Wednesday Feb. 11-Tuesday Feb. 17

The premise of the novel "Red Alert", on which "Dr. Strangelove" (1964) is based is serious; the built-in contradictions of   '   ''
Stanley Kubrick
'ional su

Our first program, January 1981, with calligraphy by Suzanne Rexford-Winston.

Paramount Pictures similarly discarded Louis Malle's *Atlantic City*, with Burt Lancaster's career-capping performance as an aging gangster. The film is now considered a modern classic; it's hard to imagine that it was once perceived by its distributor as a flop to write off. It seemed the film's uneasy mix of comedy, character study, and thriller spooked Paramount (the *New York Times* critic Vincent Canby referred to its "odd, sometimes disturbing juxtapositions of image, mood and event"). The company did not know how to market this unclassifiable film and, after a lackluster opening earlier that April, consigned it to the scrap heap. That turned out to be us. We were delighted to rescue this abandoned film and watch it become our most successful film of the summer.

"Abandoned" is not too strong a word. Taking off on the phrase (and the 1964 Italian film of that name) "seduced and abandoned," *Produced and Abandoned* is the title of a 1990 anthology of film reviews published by the National Society of Film Critics. *Atlantic City* was one of the ninety-two films featured in the book. I count forty of those ninety-two that played during our first decade at the Savoy. As the anthology's editor, Michael Sragow, wrote, "What venturesome audiences are finding is that commercial failures are funnier, sexier, more dashing—as well as more penetrating and more provocative—than their money-making counterparts."

I had been reading the *New York Times* movie page since I was ten. Now it was for more than mere amusement. Reviews such as the glowing one in the *Times* for *Atlantic City* (Canby had concluded his review by calling the film a "rich, gaudy cinema trip") sent up an early alert signal: let's keep our eye on this one. Gary and I had faith in our audience; even if a film proved a commercial flop elsewhere, it just might get an appreciative audience in Montpelier. Sometimes we were dead wrong, as with Lamont Johnson's *Cattle Annie and Little Britches* (a western with the ever-adventurous Burt Lancaster), *Chilly Scenes of Winter* (Joan Micklin Silver's adaptation of an Anne Tyler novel), and *Comfort and Joy* (Bill Forsyth's Scottish comedy). Now and then, though, we struck gold with cast-off films: *Atlantic City*; the future cult film *Repo Man*, directed by Alex Cox; *Dreamchild*, a British tale about Alice Liddell (the "real" Alice in Wonderland), directed by Gavin Millar; and Patricia Rozema's offbeat Canadian comedy *I've Heard the Mermaids Singing*.

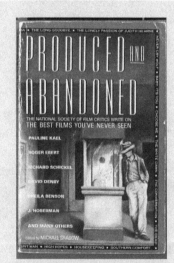

We showed many of the films featured in this book.

But the real box-office winners, we discovered, were the films from Australia and New Zealand. The opening of the Savoy came just after the start of what was to be called "the

Down Under New Wave." Although several of these films are listed in *Produced and Abandoned*, for us they were almost always hits.[20]

Starting with our almost-opening film, Gillian Armstrong's *My Brilliant Career*, that first year featured Peter Weir's 1977 *Picnic at Hanging Rock* (considered the official start of the New Wave) and Bruce Beresford's *Breaker Morant*, based on a historical incident involving Australian soldiers in the Boer War. The Down Under films were foreign, yet in English; they had accessible stories, yet featured an exotic landscape of desert outback and eucalyptus forest, photographed vividly. They also had spectacular costume and production design to ogle and new stars to admire: Judy Davis, Bryan Brown, Sam Neill, Wendy Hughes, and Bruno Lawrence.

The combination of Australian films and newer foreign fare tilted our programming from mainly revival to mainly contemporary by the end of our first year. While our first six months featured twice as many Lightning Ridge classics (such as *Top Hat*, *Rebecca*, and *Some Like It Hot*) as current films, by the start of January 1982, the ratio was in the other direction.

We were also beginning to establish relationships with some of the smaller film distributors. I especially enjoyed dealing with Nancy Gerstman and Emily Russo at Zeitgeist Films, Don Krim at Kino International, and Fran Spielman at First Run Features. Ken Eisen was a friend who, with colleagues, operated Railroad Square Cinema in Waterville, Maine; now the collective had just started its own company, Shadow Distribution, which supplied us with several excellent films.

These relationships meant the Savoy was able to play films such as the Oscar winner for Best Foreign Language Film of 1980, *Moscow Does Not Believe in Tears*, and the winner for Best Documentary that year, *From Mao to Mozart: Isaac Stern in China*. It was a mutually beneficial arrangement: just as theater-chain companies would not give these smaller distributors the time of day, Paramount et al. would have laughed at us if we tried to book films like *E.T.*

---

[20] The exceptions were two violent-uprising-against-white-settlers films, the Australian *The Chant of Jimmie Blacksmith* and the New Zealand film *Utu*. Both films are brilliantly done but graphically violent.

We learned, though, to our dismay, that excellent reviews in the national press did not automatically translate into ticket sales. This was especially true for foreign films. During these early years, there were local reviewers—Gene Novogrodsky and Kate Winslow in the *Times Argus*, Norma Jane Skjold in the *Washington World*, Barry Snyder and Susan Green in various Burlington outlets—who wrote perceptively and enthusiastically about the Savoy's international selections. But some films, it seemed, were just too foreign—or perhaps they were too "depressing," a term that I came to understand as "too involved with difficult real-life issues." A film about a troubled Quebecois family (*Les Bons Debarras*)? A film about Japanese migrants in the Brazilian coffee fields (*Gaijin*)? A film about a Polish "model worker" who becomes disillusioned with the regime (*Man of Marble*)? "No, thanks," said our audience en masse.

The challenges of marketing these films came home to us in early 1982 with an excellent Swiss film called *The Boat Is Full*. Set during World War II, the film deals with Switzerland's reluctance (despite its vaunted reputation for "neutrality") to admit Jewish refugees. We knew it would be a hard sell, so we made sure to get reviews from the *Times Argus*, the *Washington World*, and the *Vermont Vanguard*, a Burlington weekly. Despite their positive reviews, the film was a commercial disappointment. I learned recently that the same thing had happened in Burlington, an hour away. University of Vermont film professor Frank Manchel persuaded theater owner Merrill Jarvis to show *The Boat Is Full*. A few days after it opened, Frank got a call from Merrill: "The boat may be full, but the theater is empty."

But hope springs eternal, especially when one's options are limited. Once in a while—just often enough to give us confidence—a foreign film or one with a difficult theme did well. The Canadian feature *Ticket to Heaven*, about a young man enmeshed in a Moonie-like cult, was one. We could count on the Australians: there's hardly a more difficult subject than the senseless death of thousands in World War I, yet Peter Weir's *Gallipoli* drew appreciative crowds. Another was the poignant documentary *Best Boy*, filmmaker Ira Wohl's tribute to his developmentally delayed cousin Philly.

". . .but the theater is empty."

One of many Down Under hits in the early days.

Best Boy was our first hit with a documentary. It was followed over the next few years by more successes whose receptions both buoyed and puzzled us. *Lord of the Dance*, about the making of a Tibetan sand mandala (not to be confused with Michael Flatley's Irish dance extravaganza!); *Matter of Heart*, the life of Carl Jung; and *Waterwalker*, which followed Canadian canoeist Bill Mason, each drew significantly larger crowds than we expected—larger even than many higher-profile films we had shown. Their success made us ever more eager to seek out documentaries that might hit the "sweet spot" for Central Vermont's unique audience.

The opening of the Savoy also coincided with a new trend that thrilled us: the rise of the independent American film. *Return of the Secaucus Seven*, which we showed in April 1981, was the harbinger of exciting films to come. The writer and director John Sayles had two well-received novels to his name, *Pride of the Bimbos* and *Union Dues*. He had also written several sci-fi and horror scripts for Roger Corman's New World Pictures (*Piranha*, *Alligator*, and *Battle Beyond the Stars*). *The Return of the Secaucus Seven* began life as what Sayles called a "portfolio film." His idea was that for relatively little money ($45,000), he would have something to show executives in Hollywood in order to secure production money to finance a more expensive film. The cast consisted of several of his Williams College friends and actors Sayles knew from acting in summer stock. The film he wrote and directed is set at a New Hampshire reunion of former political activists who are now facing their thirties and wondering what's next. Sayles has said he didn't realize that the film was going to strike such a resonant chord among moviegoers who were facing similar crises in their own lives. Vincent Canby, in the *New York Times*, called it "an honest, fully realized movie." Even though the acting was uneven (David Strathairn as a townie stole the show) and it was clearly a low-budget effort, its rueful humor and ragged charm made it a surprise hit for its distributor, Libra Films.

The Return of the Secaucus Seven gave us our biggest crowds since opening week. The Williams College tie that provided Sayles with some of his cast also gave us our first featured guest: Bruce MacDonald, one of the lead actors in the film, was a Williams College friend of Montpelier resident Phil Dodd. Bruce was eager to promote the film any way he could. An enthusiastic audience kept a question-and-answer session going for almost an hour.[21] Years later, Bruce's daughter Jessica (who appears as a toddler in Sayles' film) moved to Montpelier and worked at Downstairs Video.

Our next "indie" hit was Victor Nuñez' *Gal Young 'Un*. This film, our first feature in January 1982, was based on a short story by Marjorie Kinnan Rawlings and was shot entirely in Florida with unknown actors. Then, it seemed, the floodgates opened: Spike Lee's *She's Gotta Have It*, Jim Jarmusch's *Stranger Than Paradise*, and the Coen brothers' debut, *Blood Simple*, heralded a new era. Small and savvy new distributors popped up—Miramax, Cinecom, Vestron, and others. We experienced

[21] Other guests followed Bruce as the years went on. When we showed David Mamet's first film, the thriller *House of Games* in 1987, he and his then-wife Lindsay Crouse, who starred in the film, came to speak at one show. Director Jay Craven made many trips to the Savoy, including one with actress Tantoo Cardinal, who starred in *Where the Rivers Flow North*. Actress Johanne-Marie Tremblay traveled from Quebec to speak about Denys Arcand's unconventional drama *Jesus of Montreal*.

ENDS TUESDAY

"A JOY TO WATCH!"
ONE OF THE YEAR'S
TEN BEST!
TIME MAGAZINE

Return of the
Secaucus 7
A film by John Sayles

TODAY: 4:15, 6:30, 8:45
SENIOR CITIZENS
$1.50 AT ALL TIMES

THE SAVOY THEATER
26 Main Street/Montpelier 229-0509

The Return of the Secaucus Seven was our first indie hit.

an unusual phenomenon: being able to show many potentially successful films.

But troubling developments outside our control started affecting us in 1982. There was now a six-screen theater in Burlington, the Nickelodeon, devoted to foreign and independent films. As a result, we lost part of our audience that lived closer to Burlington. By 1984, the Capitol Theater—our neighbor and competitor in town—had four screens (shortly to become five). The idea of starting a one-screen theater, as we did in 1980, now seemed quaint. A friend asked if we were about to go into the buggy-whip business.

And then there was the "fantastic new concept," as it was advertised in the *Times Argus* in 1981: the video store. Although the first video store officially opened in Los Angeles in 1977, it wasn't until July 1984 that one opened in Montpelier, just around the corner, on State Street. For a theater like ours, where showing revivals was still part of the Savoy's plan, this was a terrifying concept. In addition to the increasing competition from multiplex theaters, customers could now stage their own Hitchcock or Welles festival right at home. Our target audience could also simply wait six months until the newest feature came out in Beta or VHS.

Our plight was no secret. My friend and "comrade-in-arts" Jay Craven, who had been bringing high-quality films to the St. Johnsbury area, wrote an op-ed for the *Times Argus* blaming the proliferation of videos for the Savoy's travails. He compared the predicament faced by independent theaters like the Savoy to the declining fortunes of Vermont's dairy farmers once bulk milk tanks were introduced in the 1950s.[22] He added, "The video is fine for catching up on missed or forgotten movies, but it is no substitute for primary film viewing . . . It also dwarfs the filmmaker's expression by taking it out of the audience environment for which it was intended."

Too late, we realized that the Savoy might have had greater success as a nonprofit, tax-exempt organization from the beginning. We started to explore the possibility of converting to such a structure, but as we discovered, the Reagan administration's hostility toward the nonprofit sector (especially in the arts) was too great an obstacle.[23] In 1983, Gary and I developed an alternative idea to the nonprofit/tax-exempt conundrum. We created a separate 501(c)(3)—i.e., tax-exempt—organization that could accept donations, apply for grants, and promote even more financially risky film programming, while paying rental to the Savoy. The new organization's name, suggested by Montpelier filmmaker Dorothy Tod, was "Focus on Film."[24]

The programs sponsored by that group included a showing of the Spanish Civil War documentary *The Good Fight*, with two veterans of the Abraham Lincoln Brigade in attendance; a four-film French-language series and two Spanish-language series, both done in conjunction with local high school language departments; and a showing of Robert Richter's *In Our Hands*, which documented the historic June 12, 1982, Rally for Nuclear Disarmament in New York City. In 1985, Focus on Film presented its first week-long series, a Yiddish Culture Film Festival.

---

[22]Historian Mark Bushnell has written, "Beginning in 1952, milk handlers from Massachusetts and Vermont began pushing farmers to install stainless steel bulk tanks. The new tanks made it easier for the handlers to collect milk, thereby cutting their costs. The cost of the shiny new tanks, however, was borne by farmers. Or in thousands of instances, not borne by farmers who instead went out of business, having decided the investment was too expensive."

[23]During the 1970s, both the National Endowment for the Arts and the National Endowment for the Humanities had funded projects, like documentary films on historical subjects, that were now considered by the Reaganites to be too left-of-center.

[24]Besides Dorothy Tod, Focus on Film's board members were Richard Hathaway, Gene Novogrodsky, Norman Bloom, Robert Brower, Larry Mires, Martha Rich, and Chris Wood.

But the early successes of Focus on Film were not nearly enough to turn the tide. In an article in the *Times Argus* marking our third anniversary, Gary identified yet another obstacle to drawing large (or large enough) audiences: the perception that we were "too countercultural." He elaborated, "I wouldn't be surprised if there's still this 'alternative' aspect, even though we show some very commercial films . . . We don't want to be labeled, and we don't want to keep away any part of a potential audience."

By early 1986, we were faced with ever-declining attendance and a gloomy future for the Savoy. We were also at the mercy of the boom-and-bust cycle of the calendar year, without a guarantee that the summer or Christmas season would produce films that could pay for the slower months (invariably March, May, and October).

It was at this point that we had a fateful meeting with David Wise, a good friend who had some valuable experience in marketing. His advice stunned us: "Close the theater!"

But there was more to it . . .

TRAILER:
EXPLORING MY JEWISH CULTURAL
HERITAGE THROUGH FILM

The origins of Focus on Film's first major event, a Yiddish Culture Film Festival in November 1985, can be traced back to my Yiddish-speaking maternal grandparents, who lived with us in Yonkers. They often listened to the Yiddish programs on the radio station WEVD, the New York station that was founded in 1927 by the Socialist Party of America; its call letters honored the Socialist activist Eugene Victor Debs. Although my grandparents inhabited a "Jewish world," neither they nor my parents were actually religious. My parents' entire social circle—mainly public school teachers and artists—were secular Jews, and I never set foot in the synagogue on our street until it was time for my friends' bar mitzvahs. When I moved to rural Vermont in the fall of 1970, I quickly found that life in Yankee New England, especially at Christmastime, sharpened my sense of Jewish identity.

In the late 1970s, I hosted a folk and traditional music radio show—oddly enough, on a station called WDEV (decidedly not named for Debs, Eugene Victor). In 1978, a record arrived at the station that immediately stood apart from the volumes of Cajun, Irish, and other ethnic music I had amassed: *East Side Wedding*, by the California-based band called Klezmorim. I recognized it immediately as the kind of music that accompanied *The Forward Hour* and *The Jewish Philosopher* on my grandparents' radio.

A few years later, some friends and I formed Vermont's first—and for many years only—klezmer band, Nisht Geferlach. I had suggested that name, which was a Yiddish phrase ("Don't worry about it!") my grandmother often used. My growing interest in the roots of klezmer music led to a friendship with Henry Sapoznik, one of the mainstays of the klezmer music revival of the 1980s. Henry was at this time the curator of the sound archives at the YIVO Institute for Jewish Learning in Manhattan. When I mentioned to Henry my hazy idea about a Yiddish-language film festival in Montpelier, he immediately put me in touch with Richard Siegel of the National Foundation for Jewish Culture. That organization ultimately co-sponsored our week-long Yiddish Culture Film Festival in November 1985.

The films were surprisingly easy to find, since the Brandeis University–based Center for Jewish Film had an impressive collection. Henry came to the event to introduce and discuss *Image Before My Eyes*, a documentary on pre–World War II Jewish cultural life in Poland, for which he had arranged the music. Henry's colleague at the YIVO Institute, the librarian Zachary Baker, spoke on the melodrama *A Brivele Der Maman* (A Letter to Mother), and my friend Avram Patt, the singer in Nisht Geferlach, spoke about *Yidl Mitn Fidl* (Yidl With His Fiddle), starring Molly Picon as a traveling klezmer musician. Aaron Lansky, who had recently turned his passion for collect-ing old and neglected Yiddish books into the National Yiddish Book Center in Amherst, Massachusetts, was our speaker for Maurice Schwartz's film version of Sholem Aleichem's short story collection, *Tevye the Dairyman* (the source material for *Fiddler on the Roof*).

FOCUS ON FILM
presents a
YIDDISH CULTURE FILM FESTIVAL

Maurice Schwartz as TEVYE (photo courtesy National Center for Jewish Film)

**SATURDAY, NOVEMBER 9
THRU
THURSDAY, NOVEMBER 14, 1985**

1985: Focus on Film's first major venture.

The festival was an enormous success on many levels: the substantial attendance, the excellent films, the illuminating speakers, and the sense of a vibrant Jewish community in central Vermont. As I had written in the booklet that accompanied the festival, "Many members of my generation are turning our memories of what was quaint and mysterious into a search for what is significant and alive. This festival is part of that process of discovery."

CHAPTER 11

THANK YOU, DAVID WISE

David Wise, of Montpelier, was an accomplished painter, photographer, graphic artist, and all-around visionary thinker. As both a movie buff and a friend, he was someone we called upon occasionally to discuss the Savoy's place in the Central Vermont community. I don't know if "thinking outside the box" was in common parlance in the early 1980s, but that would be a perfect description of David's problem-solving approach. He always challenged us to look beyond our narrow vision, to imagine how others perceived the Savoy, and to find imaginative solutions to our difficulties.

The brilliant David Wise, who conceived the Savoy's membership campaign.

When Gary and I told David about our mounting problems—demographic shifts, the video juggernaut, declining audiences, our diminishing bank account—his advice was immediate. "Close the theater—and announce you won't reopen until you've raised a certain amount of money." He continued, "If you send a fundraising appeal to the people on your mailing list, they will be the only ones who know you're in trouble. If you close, the entire world will know!" In the meantime, he suggested, come up with a plan for continuing support, aimed at all our patrons who had told us that they counted on us to be there.

At that time, David was working for Time-Life publications, designing a direct-marketing package for their books. "You've got something at the Savoy that money can't buy," he told us. We leaned forward, eager to hear what that X factor might be. "It's the perception that the Savoy is a nonprofit organization!" David convinced us that the community viewed the Savoy as an arts organization rather than a downtown business.

That argument sold us. We worked with him to devise a yearly membership plan, with certain perks for each tier, whether two free admissions or free popcorn

Front page of the *Times Argus*, April 1986; *Hail Mary* is appropriate.

for the year. We went up through the tiers this way, from $25 to $50 to $100 to $250. We suggested capping the membership categories at $750 (it seemed so exorbitant!), but David challenged us. "No! You're thinking too small. Put in a $1,000 category for a lifetime membership, free admission and free popcorn." We swallowed hard and followed his advice.

The Savoy's closing, on May 2 1986, was timed for our slowest period of the year.[25] It was on the front page of the *Times Argus*, above the fold. I was quoted as saying that we had sent two thousand letters to patrons on the mailing list. Said the *Argus*: "In the middle of the

---

[25]One glorious spring day, I gazed across the street from the theater and composed a seasonal haiku: "Crabapple blossoms/At City Hall signify/Savoy's empty seats."

letter in bold letters, it states that if the Savoy deficit is eliminated, it will reopen on June 20." Gary told the reporter, "We have the option of cutting our losses and quitting, or doing something drastic. We're going to give the community a chance to respond." Our friend John Miller at Sign Design painted the front window with a fundraising message, complete with the requisite fundraising thermometer.

Camera, Lights, Action!
Savoy Theater To Reopen

By GAYLE HANSON
Times Argus Staff

MONTPELIER — Although they say the "struggle is not yet over," Savoy Theatre owners Rick Winston and Gary Ireland announced today that over $20,000 had been raised through a membership drive and benefit concert, and the financially troubled theatre would reopen on June 20.

"We knew we were taking a risk by closing, but the depth and breadth of support in the community has been incredible," Winston said.

Winston indicated support for the theatre came from throughout the state and

of the money will be used to pay off accumulated debts, there is enough left over to help subsidize future programming.

Winston and Ireland plan to use some of the many suggestions they received to help program special events, and film series at the theatre. They also hope to collaborate with other organizations in the community.

The theatre will reopen with the highly acclaimed film "Turtle Diary" starring Glenda Jackson. Winston said

After being closed for a month...

Within the week we had three lifetime memberships, and within the month we had received enough other memberships to feel secure in reopening. Although David was right on several counts, he was nevertheless amazed at our rate of response. He hadn't told us beforehand, but he now explained that the rule of thumb on direct-mail response was around eight percent. Ours was closer to eighty percent.

As a result, the Savoy went into the summer of 1986 on a firm footing. It also helped that we showed three hit films in a row: the "produced and abandoned" Albert Brooks film *Lost in America*, now considered one of the great comedies of the so-called "Me Decade"; John Sayles' sci-fi/romantic comedy/political critique *The Brother From Another*

Planet, and another unlikely Australian crowd-pleaser, Paul Cox's *Man of Flowers*.

The membership program became the foundation of the Savoy's finances in the years that followed. Our accountant noted with some amazement that each year he could count on the membership line in our profit/loss statement to make up close to the exact difference between breaking even and losing money.

From early on, a part of the yearly membership letter—along with the membership form and a free popcorn coupon—was a page titled "Winners and Losers." Here, in graph form, was a list of our ten most successful films and the ten that drew the slimmest crowds. At first, the intention was simply to be transparent about the challenges of operating an art cinema far from major metropolitan areas. Our audience had demonstrated that they had an emotional stake in the success of the theater; the "Winners and Losers" was a way of including them as much as we could.

But the "Winners and Losers" became an unlikely membership-marketing tool as well. We started to hear patrons say, "I was going to give $25, but after seeing that my favorite film of the year had tanked, I gave $75." The favorite film might have been an American indie like *Parting Glances*, one of the first films about the AIDS epidemic; a British historical drama like *Another Country*, with Rupert Everett and Colin Firth; or a Dutch thriller like *The Vanishing*. Advertising our failures may have struck some people as perverse, but it paid off in terms of retaining faithful members.

The membership campaign inspired by David Wise heralded a new era for the Savoy. Our relationship with the Central Vermont audience had evolved: the film lovers who supported us were not just "customers," but community members who felt a sense of ownership in the theater. They were now invested in our future. Optimism had been in short supply for those last few years, but now Gary and I could imagine better times ahead.

CHAPTER 12

THE "CULTURAL SPEAKEASY" DOWNSTAIRS

By the mid-1980s, the effects of the video store phenomenon became impossible to ignore. Our industry friend Jeffrey Jacobs put it succinctly: "The rise of the video store devalued the repertory cinema." But as much as this development spelled challenging times for the Savoy, I had a grudgingly positive attitude about some aspects of this technological advance.

The emerging video market—especially as practiced by discriminating companies like Facets, Inc.—meant that a large number of hard-to-find films now could be located, rented, and enjoyed at home. In the mid-1980s, Andrea and I broke down and purchased a video player. If I remember correctly, the first film we watched was the British postwar comedy *Passport to Pimlico*, which I had chased for years. It was only the small screen, but it was better than nothing.

As we fretted over the increased competition from video stores, our Northampton friend John Morrison looked at things differently. In 1986, John and Richard Pini had opened Pleasant Street Video, right next door to their Pleasant Street Cinema. "You should think about starting your own store," John advised. "People will take out videos five nights a week, but still want to see the latest film on the screen on Friday and Saturday."

That was certainly something to think about. We didn't even have far to look for another space, since we already had a completely empty basement that housed only our bathrooms. Some patrons confessed that they avoided making bathroom trips since the cavernous downstairs space was "creepy." Now we could convert this dank, forbidding space into a brightly-lit, welcoming room.

In 1988, with support from one of our projectionists, Rhonda Beardsworth, we started making plans for our own video store. Like the theater, it would highlight classic, foreign, independent, and documentary films. Children's films, too, would be selected with care. Once again, John and Richard gave us the benefit of their Pleasant Street experience, explaining the basics of video purchase and how to set up a coherent system for rentals.

Downstairs Video opens in January of 1989.

The name of the store? That was an easy one. Andrea pointed out that no matter what we named it, people would always refer to it as "downstairs from (or at) the Savoy." "Downstairs Video" it was, with an appropriately catchy logo designed by Tim Newcomb, a Montpelier artist already establishing his name as a graphic designer and political cartoonist. Instead of figuring out the dimensions of a projection booth and concession stand, now the challenge for Jim Donnon, David Smith, and crew was to build video racks and storage drawers.

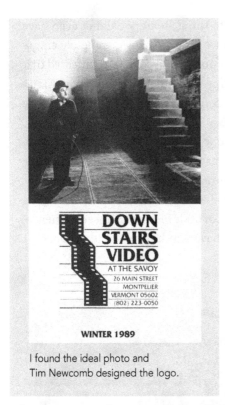

DOWN STAIRS VIDEO

AT THE SAVOY

26 MAIN STREET
MONTPELIER
VERMONT 05602
(802) 223-0050

WINTER 1989

I found the ideal photo and Tim Newcomb designed the logo.

We settled on seven hundred titles to start, given our limited space. That number sounded like a lot at first, but once Gary and I came up with a list of must-haves (from Billy Wilder and Alfred Hitchcock to Ingmar Bergman and Akira Kurosawa), the choices became progressively more difficult. Of course, we should have oddball films that did well at the Savoy, like the Dutch thriller *The Fourth Man* and the Australian romance *Lonely Hearts*. But did that mean having only five Howard Hawks films instead of ten? Or *Little Women* and *Pride and Prejudice* but not *David Copperfield*? Five Czech films but only one Polish one? It was a challenging process but nevertheless thrilling, especially when we visualized all those titles, representing the best of seventy years of cinema, in one intimate space.

A major video wholesaler, Artec, turned out to be in our general neighborhood (South Burlington). It was a dizzying experience to set foot in its warehouse with the goal of bringing back hundreds of titles. We also quickly discovered, as we had in the theater, that there were smaller distributors specializing in the older American classics, foreign titles, and children's films. One such find was a company in Connecticut called Weston Woods; its concentration was producing excellent animated versions of classic children's books such as *Doctor Desoto* and *Mike Mulligan and His Steam Shovel*.

After years of poring over film catalogs, I now had a chance to produce one. I spent hours happily occupied in putting together our forty-page listing, illustrated with film stills, detailing our seven hundred titles with year, running time, director, genre, and a single-sentence—sometimes a long sentence—description. On our introductory page, we said, "We think you will agree that the offerings present a balance and focus that will set Downstairs Video apart from other video outlets."

Although we did note the genre of the particular film in the catalog, the physical space—unlike most video stores—was arranged not into

Bad Day at Black Rock

THE AUTOBIOGRAPHY OF MISS JANE PITTMAN

1974   110 min   J. Korty   DRA

The moving life story of a 110-year-old woman (played remarkably by Cicely Tyson) who was born into slavery and lived to take part in the 1960's civil rights movement.

BAD DAY AT BLACK ROCK

1954   81 min   J. Sturges   DRA

A one-armed stranger arrives in a small western town and discovers a guilty secret. A tense and socially conscious mystery with Spencer Tracy, Robert Ryan, Lee Marvin, and Ernest Borgnine.

BADLANDS

1973   95 min   T. Malick   DRA

In Malick's stunning directorial debut, Sissy Spacek and Martin Sheen play two young outcasts who fall in love and go on a killing rampage through the Midwest.

BAGDAD CAFE

1988   91 min   P. Adlon   COM

One of the most exhilerating comedies in recent years stars Marianne Sagebrecht as a German tourist stranded in the Mojave Desert who befriends a black woman who runs a truckstop-cafe. An utter delight, also starring Jack Palance.

BALLAD OF GREGORIO CORTEZ

1982   105 min   R. Young   DRA

The true story of Gregorio Cortez, a turn-of-the-century farmer who kills a sheriff due to a language misunderstanding and is hunted by the Texas Rangers. A highly acclaimed American independent film, starring Edward Olmos.

BANANAS

1971   81 min   W. Allen   COM

The hilarious story of Fielding Mellish, a meek and mild products tester in New York who finds himself a rebel leader in South America.

BARFLY

1987   100 min   B. Schroeder   COM

A hard-edged yet warmly funny story of an alcoholic writer (Mickey Rourke) who prefers to loll in the anonymity and excess of Skid Row bars. Loosely based on the life of Charles Bukowski, who wrote the screenplay.

BEING THERE

1979   130 min   H. Ashby   COM

A sublimely funny and bitingly satiric comedy featuring Peter Sellers as a simple-minded gardner whose only knowledge of the world is through television.

BELIZAIRE THE CAJUN

1986   113 min   G. Petre   DRA

One of the first American films to deal seriously with the Cajun milieu of southern Louisiana, Glen Petre's film stars Armand Assante as a Cajun healer during the mid 1800's.

BERNICE BOBS HER HAIR

1982   52 min   J. Silver   COM

A charming adaptation of the F. Scott Fitzgerald story by Joan Micklin Silver with Shelley Duvall as the girl who wants to be up-to-date. Also starring Bud Cort.

THE BEST YEARS OF OUR LIVES

1946   170 min   W. Wyler   DRA

Winner of eight Academy Awards, this sensitive film focuses on the problems of three World War II soldiers when they return home. The marvelous cast includes Frederic March, Dana Andrews, Myrna Loy, and Theresa Wright.

BINGO LONG'S TRAVELING ALL-STARS

1976   111 min   J. Badham   COM

The comedy-adventure story of a group of barnstorming players in the 1930's Negro Baseball League stars James Earl Jones, Richard Pryor, and Billy Dee Williams. Some think it's the best baseball film yet.

THE BIRDS

1963   119 min   A. Hitchcock   DRA

Alfred Hitchcock used Daphne DuMaurier's story as a starting point for his own terrifying vision of a small town terrorized by hundreds of birds. With Tippi Hedren, Rod Taylor.

BIRDY

1984   120 min   A. Parker   DRA

Matthew Modine stars as a pigeon fancier who withdraws into a bird-centered fantasy world after a Vietnam War trauma; Nicolas Cage is the buddy who tries desparately to help his friend. An unusual and moving film.

BLACK LIKE ME

1964   107 min   C. Lerner   DRA

James Whitmore stars as John Howard Griffin, who dyed his skin so that he might experience prejudice first-hand in the South.

BLADE RUNNER

1982   114 min   R. Scott   SCI

Harrison Ford stars in this futuristic thriller, battling androids in space-age Los Angeles. From the sci-fi novel by Philp K. Dick.

BLOOD SIMPLE

1983   96 min   E. & J. Coen   MYS

This critically acclaimed thriller set in rural Texas combines chilling suspense with offbeat humor and a spectacular visual style.

BLUE VELVET

1986   120 min   D. Lynch   MYS

David Lynch's controversial, surreal mystery set in an all-American town where violence and perversion lurk under the surface. Starring Isabella Rosselini and Dennis Hopper.

BONNIE AND CLYDE

1967   111 min   A. Penn   DRA

Faye Dunaway and Warren Beatty star as the two outlaws who, to their own amaze-ment, became folk heroes during the Depression. With Gene Hackman, Michael J. Pollard, and Estelle Parsons.

A page from our original catalog.

"Mystery," "Adventure," "Romance," but instead by nationality. The United States section was huge, naturally, compared to the Eastern European shelf—but how many other video stores even had an Eastern European section? We did make an exception for our Children's Corner, which had not only videos but a play area and picture books. Some of those picture books came from my own childhood collection.

We proudly unveiled the dungeon-turned-video-store in January 1989. In one sense, that opening date represented fortuitous timing. Had we opened a year earlier, we would have had to order our films in both VHS and Betamax formats. The companies that produced these incompatible products had been fighting for control of the home video market for the previous decade. We had remained blissfully ignorant of that struggle; by the time we were ready to buy our stock, the dust had settled and VHS was the clear winner.[26]

Our first computer was still three years in the future. The features of the seat-of-our-pants system of recording rentals and late fees were a clipboard, metal file boxes, lined index cards, and colored metal tabs. God forbid your shift was a day after another staff person who had terrible handwriting, which invariably became more illegible the busier we were. We could count on the weekends being busy times, but also the day before Thanksgiving and Christmas. We'd hear, "I want two films to keep the kids occupied, a few we can all watch together . . . and oh yes, nothing R-rated for my parents." Someone joked we should open a sideline business of family counseling.

The other busy days we could rely on were the day before, or the morning of, a predicted snowstorm. On one Saturday morning in partic-ular, the checkout line went all the way up the stairs to the lobby of the

[26]The Betamax story was a harbinger of the technological advances that determined the short life cycle of the video store phenomenon itself. For a while in the early '90s, it looked as though LaserDiscs were going to be the wave of the future; we let Pleasant Street Video be our canary in the coal mine and decided not to follow that lead after the results were in. Then we heard about the new technology called DVDs. We stuck one toe in the water by buying around twenty of the popular titles in that format. Then, the deluge. With each succeeding Christmas, more people were receiving DVD players as presents. Soon, we stopped buying new titles in VHS. First the high-definition television (1998) and then Netflix-by-mail in the early 2000s were the early warning signs for the ultimate demise of video stores.

theater. Almost all those customers had just been to the supermarket to buy candles in case they lost electricity, and now they were picking up videos in case it stayed on but they were still housebound.

Our patchwork system finally gave way to our first Mac in early 1992. Our Montpelier friend Paul Haskell had just started a business designing IT systems. We were his early (and appreciative) guinea pigs, as he adapted our very specific needs to a FileMaker Pro program. We could say to Paul, "What if somebody takes out a movie and pays a late fee at the same time?" and he'd get right to work on it.

We learned early to position our new release shelf front and center. When a major film like *Dances with Wolves* or *Mean Streets* (to name two of 1989's major films) opened in movie theaters, we would have loved to play them at the Savoy. But those films automatically went to the Capitol

New release shelf (left) and mini office (right).

Theater, around the corner on State Street. After all, the Capitol had established relationships with the large distributors and could play a film for months if it chose. But at Downstairs Video, those films, in VHS or later in DVD format, were available to us as they were to any other outlet, whether video store or beverage redemption center. Our very rough calculus was that the rental of three copies each of such popular films might subsidize some of the more obscure foreign language titles that we loved but that were rented only rarely.

The atmosphere at Downstairs Video was somewhat different from that of the theater upstairs. Upstairs, people bought tickets and (non-Red Dye #40) popcorn, found a seat inside, and came back out two hours later. Conversation, though lively, was often short-lived—"How's the family?" over the concession stand or "That was excellent!" on their way out. Theater staff never got to hear in more detail whether customers were moved or entertained—or even disappointed.

At Downstairs Video, however, as Andrea, who became manager in 1991, puts it, there was more physical space, but there was also metaphorical space; customers could browse for an hour or engage in film discussion with whoever was on duty. If they were impressed with a particular film they had just rented, that could lead to a half-hour conver-

Ed Wood Jr.'s cult classic *Plan 9 From Outer Space*.

sation. In that way, the space could feel more like a library than a retail store. It even had, as our friend Nona Estrin observed, the ambience of a literary salon. Another habitué, Tom Hall, called it "a cultural speakeasy:" "No one left disappointed or uninformed, because the stream of cinema on offer was so broad and welcoming."

To reinforce the idea of a library, we also installed a shelf of film books for reference or browsing. Tom Hall said he had his "own fond memories of the collection of film books which ranged in tone from august and scholarly to the deceptively trivial. I was particularly taken with a volume entitled *Kings of the Bs,* consisting of interviews with Hollywood directors who'd toiled in the field of restricted-budget second features."

This atmosphere encouraged repeat business. It also resulted in some long-standing friendships and recruiting for staff positions. One day, Andrea had a discussion with a high school student, Thomas Murphey, that led to mention of Miles Davis. She suggested that he check out Louis Malle's 1958 film *Elevator to the Gallows,* which had a haunting score by Davis. Within a year, Thomas was working behind the counter, making his own suggestions of out-of-the-way films some customers would appreciate.

Our staff—who had wide-ranging tastes themselves—got to know patrons' preferences. They came to sense who might appreciate Ed Wood's cult film *Plan 9 From Outer Space* and who would rather see Ingmar Bergman's *Fanny and Alexander.*[27]

The staff also knew enough to warn customers away from a film whose display box was misleading. Whatever exaggeration studios used in advertising a theatrical-release film was even more extreme when it came to selling videos. Very few customers wanted to rent a "depressing" film—which I took to mean anything that actively depicted disturbing social and political issues. Miramax studios, which had a well-deserved reputation for discriminating taste in film distribution, had a video division whose copywriters twisted themselves into knots to describe any film as "feel good" even if it dealt with racism, unemployment, or the Holocaust.

It was clear that customers watching a film at home brought different standards than they did for moviegoing. A video rental was

---

[27]Staff member Michael Macomber recalled that "I learned more about film than I ever did in my two years at an actual film school. I systematically worked my way through the films on the shelves, each carefully categorized by its country of origin. Some of my favorite films at the time were *Un Coeur en Hiver, Walking and Talking,* and *Vanya on 42nd Street,* anything directed by Krzysztof Kieslowski, Tom DiCillo, Jane Campion, Nicole Holefcener, or Jim Jarmusch, and anything starring Catherine Keener, Liev Schreiber, Julianne Moore, and John Turturro."

a fraction of the night-out-at-the-movies cost ($2.50 versus $15 for two in 1990, not counting dinner and/or a babysitter); why not take a chance on an unknown quantity—especially when it came recommended by one of the staff? We were pleased when films like the Danish coming-of-age drama *Twist and Shout* or James Gray's thriller *Little Odessa*, both of which had flopped upstairs, found an appreciative audience downstairs.

Andrea and the staff were always eager to recommend such titles, but sometimes all a patron wanted was two hours of respite from work or news headlines. After perhaps the hundredth person came in (often on a Friday night after work) saying, "I need a comedy," we printed a sheet headed, "Looking for a Comedy?" Here we broke the films down into categories: the ones I remember are "Older Classics" (*Bringing Up Baby*), "Sophisticated British" (*The Man in the White Suit*), and my favorite, "Stupid but Funny" (*The Jerk* and *Young Frankenstein*). When it was my turn to take a video store shift, I'd often run Mel Brooks' *Young Frankenstein* on the television behind the counter (the TV was a must-have, said our friends at Pleasant Street Video); Andrea's tastes ran more to *Guys and Dolls*. Both films made for many a conversational icebreaker.

We did our best to encourage adventurous renting. On certain days, we had a two-for-one special, but only if the second one was a foreign language film. On Bastille Day, all French titles were free. A special display near the front counter changed every month, highlighting some of our unusual titles. The staff often came up with ideas for this shelf that went beyond the usual "Great Comedies" or "Thrilling Murder Mysteries." Some displays that I remember were "Great Pairs" (*Thelma and Louise, Harry and Tonto, Burke and Wills*) and one that just had a sign proclaiming "The" (*The Shining, The Uninvited, The Killing,* and other two-word titles).

After two years it became clear that certain obscure titles were simply going to sit unrented. We culled roughly two hundred of these films and put them in a new section we called the "Archive." Here, all films—like the early Kurosawa *No Regrets for Our Youth* and the Mexican historical epic *Cabeza De Vaca*—were one dollar each. One of our most loyal customers, Marion Gray, made it a point to work her way through the archive section backward, starting with *Z*, a thriller by the Greek/French director Costa-Gavras.

The Archive section only lasted until March 11, 1992. That day almost spelled the end of the entire video store, as well.

Sandy Macys/Times Argus

Gary Ireland and Rick Winston stand in front of the sign of the original Savoy Theater, which was open from 1908 to 1914 at the same Main Street location.

Savoy Uses Boom In VCRs To Keep Customers Satisfied

By BETH HOLTZMAN
Times Argus Staff

MONTPELIER — When Rick Winston and Gary Ireland opened the Savoy Theater in January 1981, their idea was to show high quality movies — classics and foreign films — which rarely, if ever, played in Vermont.

The explosion of the VCR rental market was years away, and both the Capitol Theatre in Montpelier and the Paramount in Barre still had but just one screen.

Today the Capitol has four screens, the Paramount two, and just about every convenience and grocery store rents video tapes.

And the Savoy, with its single screen, is still here, showing the high quality independent, foreign and lesser-known high studio films that regularly draw patrons from as far as away South Hero and Vershire.

Whether it's a throwback to an earlier age or on the cutting edge, the Savoy is arguably one of Central Vermont's greatest cultural success stories.

"I like to think what separates us from other theaters is that we think a lot about what we

made donations to theater to keep it alive.

At the time, Winston and Ireland pointed to the video rental market as a reason for a decline in the number of customers coming to their theater. But today the Savoy itself rents videos at its basement store, Downstairs Video.

> *"I like to think what separates us from other theaters is that we think a lot about what we want to show and we make it quality."*
>
> **—Rick Winston**

"When VCRs became popular in the mid-80s we felt it was a serious threat," Ireland said. "Attendance at our theater dropped considerably."

But after talking to other small, New England theaters that had successfully gotten into the video business, Winston, Ireland and partner Rhonda Beardsworth decided to give it try.

"Our initial contact with videos

The *Times Argus* acknowledged the changing entertainment landscape.

CHAPTER 13

"WASN'T THAT A MIGHTY STORM?"

On March 11, 1992, Andrea and I hoped for a leisurely morning. Perhaps we'd arrive at the theater by ten. But a 7:30 phone call from my brother Jon ended that plan: "You better get into town fast—the river's flooding." At the time, Jon was a member of the East Montpelier Volunteer Fire Department. He was nervously keeping an eye on weather developments. Others, like us, were blissfully unaware that an early spring thaw had threatened disaster in Montpelier, where the Winooski River flows right through downtown.

Later that year, the City of Montpelier published a commemorative book, *Ice and Water*. It described the scene that morning vividly: "The North Branch was high and the Winooski River was brimful of snowmelt and rain and chocked with floating chunks of thick winter ice. About 7 a.m., the groaning river of ice in the Winooski River shuddered to a momentous stop just downstream of the Bailey Avenue Bridge. The ice had jammed, shutting the door on the river as decisively as the closing of a bank vault. With nowhere to go, the Winooski backed up, pouring calamitously over its banks into the heart of Montpelier."

By the time we reached Upper Main Street, the downtown district had been closed to traffic. We parked at the house of friends and raced down the hill into town, terrified of what we'd find. We spied a knot of people

An ice jam caused the March 1992 flood.

at the entrance to the Savoy. As we got closer, it became clear that this was a human chain, passing our thirty-odd video storage drawers from the basement up to our office on the second floor.[28]

Ten a.m. on Main Street.

The water from the overflowing North Branch was rushing through our rear door at an ever-increasing rate. By the time Andrea, Gary, and I had arrived, there were two feet of water in the basement. Our first computer (purchased and installed just two weeks earlier) and the video storage drawers had been rescued. So were the bottom three shelves of our archive section (the top three had to be abandoned as the waters continued to rise).

Chris Wood, longtime friend of the theater and at that time a projectionist, was living downtown in an apartment overlooking the North Branch. He and his partner Mary Daeatt had been enjoying

---

[28]The VHS tapes themselves were stored in the drawers; all that was on the shelves were the four-by-seven-and-a-half-inch display boxes, made of stiff, coated cardboard. These were decorated with graphics, title, and a description of the film on the back.

their morning coffee when they noticed with dismay that the river was running the wrong way. Their first thought was "the video store!" Chris grabbed people off the street and went to work organizing the chain to salvage what was possible.

Jim Higgins, another friend, was on that brigade as well. Jim had come into Montpelier to teach at the Montpelier/U-32 Alternative Program, but learned that classes were canceled. Sensing a historic day in Montpelier, he walked around town and happened on the rescue brigade at the video store. "I got downstairs and started hauling out the drawers, handing them to whoever was on the second step," he recalled. "It was pure adrenaline. I was young and could handle the awkward sixty-pound drawers alone. And we had to do it because the waters were rising."

Jim Higgins, just a few minutes before evacuation.

Jim called that rescue operation "one of the most adventurous, exciting, and dangerous experiences of my life." He stressed the word "dangerous" because an hour after the last of the storage drawers had been hauled upstairs, someone shouted, "Hey, is the electricity turned off?" Gary then waded through the muck to turn off the power ("foolish, not heroic," he recalled). But that was only the power in the theater and video store. Our landlord, Tony Beard, and a city engineer located the main breaker to the entire building, averting an even bigger disaster.[29]

As the water continued to gush, we bid a sad farewell to the top three shelves of the archive cabinet. Before heading to drier ground, we took a final look at hundreds of display boxes floating on the rising waters. By that afternoon, the water had reached the ceiling of the store and, slightly above that, the top of the staircase leading down from the theater.

Soggy display boxes—some were salvageable.

The power was out for two more days, but the water had receded enough by the day after the flood to assess the damage. With flashlights (projectionist Norman Bloom brought in a miner's lamp for the occasion), we trudged through the silt, gathering what encrusted display boxes we could see. We stuffed them into garbage bags, distributing the bags to volunteers who took the boxes home to clean and dry.

While the manager of the building next door was frantically trying to reach her own landlord, who was on a tropical vacation, Tony and Joan Beard pitched right in, showing up in hip waders. They assured us that they would do all they could to help us reopen.

---

[29] In 1983, Tony and Joan Beard had bought the building from Jon.

The display racks were lying on their sides, but were salvageable. It was the sodden sheetrocked walls that sustained the most damage. If we wanted to resurrect the store, all our walls would have to be removed. Cue the sledgehammers and another human chain to drag the soggy mess out back to a growing mountain of trash. This was a scene that was repeated in the rear of just about every downtown business, made even more challenging with the onset of frigid temperatures.

When I try to recall that week, it is mainly the sense of shock that is still so vivid thirty years later. At the time, our dismay at what might be lost and the enormity of the task ahead were pushed to the side by the minute-by-minute demands of what had to be done immediately. I also remember the gratitude I felt, seeing the numerous volunteers who just showed up, ready to do what was asked. Gary recalled, "It was unbelievable how the community rallied on our behalf."

I was also buoyed by those—especially my brother Jon and Tony Beard—who had a clear-eyed sense of what had to happen next, whether it was to call the electrician, plumber, or insurance adjuster. For a few days anyway, as I wandered through the wreckage of the store in a zombie-like state, I was relieved of the responsibility for rational, long-range decisions.

As I've read about other crises over the years—whether 9/11 or Hurricane Katrina—I recognized not only the widespread shock and disbelief, but also the solidarity that such crises engender. No one business in Montpelier cared only about its own survival. Our fellow merchants all empathized with each other, helped each other when possible (Jane Edwards of Julio's Restaurant made sure our volunteers were fed), and embarked on the common project to bring our downtown back to life. For that whole month of March, we saw human nature at its best.

Had the flood begun just two hours earlier, while almost everyone was asleep, we would have lost our entire inventory. Then, I think, we might well have closed permanently. But we had salvaged almost all of our tapes. Downstairs Video had become a Montpelier fixture. Though rebuilding was a daunting prospect, there was never any question of closing.

Soon reconstruction began. An amazing team, headed by my brother Jon and Bruce Gratz, started work. Jon and Bruce had never met, but they were of like minds about a plan of action. Once the new walls were up and the bathroom reframed, volunteers poured in to help out with painting and cleanup. One volunteer, Mark Greenberg, while hauling out soggy sheetrock from the bathroom, asked jokingly, "See what happens when you don't jiggle the handle?"

Meanwhile, volunteers had returned the dried-out display boxes. We were then able to take stock of which boxes were salvageable and

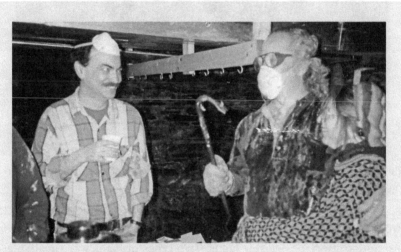

Mark Greenberg, Jon Winston, Andrea Serota: "See what happens when you don't jiggle the handle?"

which were lost forever. The next step was a trip down to Pleasant Street Video in Northampton, Massachusetts. John Morrison and I went through my list of missing boxes, checking them against his own inventory. I hauled two hundred of his display boxes in two garbage bags to the copy center across the street. More volunteers awaited my return to Montpelier, where we had a scissoring and plastic-sleeve-stuffing session. The results were often crude, but at least we had something to put back on the shelves.

The theater, which sustained much less damage than the video store, was able to open a few weeks before Downstairs Video was back in operation. It was a big night when Mira Nair's *Mississippi Masala* opened upstairs, signaling that we were back in business. Everyone was

The store had to be entirely reconstructed.

delighted —even those who had to go down the street and up the stairs to Julio's Restaurant to use the bathroom.

Throughout this period, Gary took on the considerable paper-work burden, writing detailed applications to the Small Business Administration for disaster loans. Two types of loans were available: the first covered itemized losses of equipment, and the second covered general loss of business. Gary went right to work on the first loan, doing his best to reconstruct the inventory of what was lost. He submitted the application, and the loan was promptly awarded. Our accountant then strongly advised us to apply for the second loan as well and to ask for the limit.

It was more work for Gary, but it paid off. We got that loan, too, and were able to use those funds to pay off our existing bank loan (which had a significantly higher interest rate). By summer of 1992, it was apparent—to our amazement—that the Savoy and Downstairs Video were on a firmer financial footing than we had been before the flood.

CHAPTER 14

THANK YOU, JEFFREY JACOBS

There was another change in 1992 that improved our fortunes. We hired a film buyer (or "booker"), Jeffrey Jacobs.[30] I had first met Jeffrey in film society days, when he was working for a small Manhattan film-distribution company called International Film Exchange (IFEX). He and I discovered a Vermont connection immediately: in the early 1970s, he had created and run a 16-millimeter movie theater at the Odd Fellows Hall in Waitsfield, just south of Montpelier. After a few years, he decided to leave Vermont to finish a graduate degree in film at UCLA.

By the time I reconnected with Jeffrey in the late 80s, he was the film buyer for the six-screen Angelika Film Center, the prestigious art house mecca in downtown Manhattan. Soon he started his own company, booking films for "specialty theaters" (as they came to be known) like ours.[31]

For most of the 1980s, I had done the booking for the Savoy—that is, calling the distributors and finding out what was available when, and how much they were asking for a particular film. A typical transaction went

---

[30]Our film buyer Jeffrey Jacobs should not be confused with the Jeffrey Jacobs who has owned several buildings in Montpelier.

[31]As Jeffrey explained in a talk he gave at our Green Mountain Film Festival in 2000, the term "booker" originated with the large ledger books that theaters used in order to keep track of what they showed.

Jeffrey Jacobs, our film buyer starting in 1992.

something like this: Libra Films might want a guarantee of $300 for us to play *Return of the Secaucus Seven* for a week. But there was also an agreed-upon percentage of the take, say thirty-five percent, and we'd pay whichever was higher. In the parlance of the industry, this would be known as "$300 versus thirty-five." In the case of a two-week run, a distributor might ask a $500 guarantee versus forty percent of the take the first week and thirty-five percent the second.

Most smaller distributors were easy to deal with. They were eager to get a date for their films, and their prices were usually extremely fair. We established good relationships with the knowledgeable people at Zeitgeist Films, First Run Features, Kino International, and Miramax (still in their pre-behemoth days). It was harder to get a film from a "major"—that is, Columbia, Paramount, etc. The salespeople there were just that—salespeople, hawking a product, trying to meet a monthly sales target; the notion of "film culture" was a foreign one to them.

Other problems arose as the result of the explosion of American independent films in the early 1980s. Some distributors for those films saw a potential for a mainstream audience. An established relationship with the Savoy didn't count for much when there was a potential multi-week screening down the street. I often dreaded my booking calls. I felt at a disadvantage arguing our case with seasoned (and aggressive) business pros.

Throughout the 1980s, we showed many films from Miramax Films: *Crossover Dreams*, with Ruben Blades; the coming-of-age Danish drama *Twist and Shout;* and the Canadian comedy *I've Heard the Mermaids Singing*. But as soon as their *Sex Lies and Videotape* was a surprise hit at the Sundance Film Festival in 1989, our long-standing relationship meant little to them—and even less when Miramax was bought by Walt Disney Studios in 1992.

STARTS TONIGHT
6:30 & 9:05

"A CROWNING ACHIEVEMENT
A MASTERPIECE"
- David Ansen, NEWSWEEK

★ ★ ★ ★

HOWARDS·END

THE SAVOY
THEATER
26 Main St., Montpelier   229-0509

The Merchant-Ivory film
Howards End was a big success.

The worst offenders, unfortunately, had the best films. United Artists Classics became Orion Classics in 1982 and then became Sony Pictures Classics in 1992. They were—and still are—the gold standard in discerning taste, distributing *Cyrano de Bergerac* in 1990 and *Howards End* in 1992.

But any booking with the company had to go through Michael Barker, who was brusque but ultimately fair, or Tom Bernard, a bully of the first order. He reminded me of the older kids in my high school who had made my life miserable. Unlike the supportive people working at other small distributors, Tom seemed to take a perverse pleasure in watching the Savoy struggle. I was mystified, then infuriated, by his attitude, which was so contrary to the film culture ethos I appreciated. At one point (I have mercifully forgotten the film in question), he pushed one button too many and I told him to go fuck himself, slamming down the phone. Gary looked on in amazement at my uncharacteristic behavior. I discovered after comparing notes with other specialty theater owners that I was not alone in dreading my dealings with Sony Pictures Classics.

Andrea and I would chat with Jeffrey when we stopped at the Angelika on our twice-yearly movie trips to New York City. In the winter of 1992, we sat down with him for a more serious chat. "Any time you've had enough of dealing with difficult people," he said, "I'd be happy to do it for you." He then played his winning card. "When distributors are nice to you, you've caught them on a good day. But when they're nice to me, it's because they owe me a favor."

We were ready to take Jeffrey's offer to heart. It proved immediately to be a good decision: he was able to get us a three-week Christmas run of *A River Runs Through It* from Columbia Pictures, something we'd never have achieved on our own. Jeffrey followed this up by acquiring Kenneth Branagh's *Much Ado About Nothing*, the Mexican film *Like Water for Chocolate*, and Neil Jordan's *The Crying Game*. That last film, distributed by Miramax, had received much national publicity. It would have been hard for the Savoy to book it without Jeffrey's help.

By the mid-1990s there was a significant change in the distribution landscape. Jeffrey proved to be an astute guide through this new territory. The success of Sony Pictures Classics and the purchase of Miramax by Disney opened the gates for well-funded and sophisticated distributors like October Films, Focus Features, and Paramount Classics. In a recent conversation, Jeffrey confirmed what I remembered about those days. "The mid-nineties were like no other period," he said. "There seemed to be a limitless supply of exciting and very marketable American and international films."

Sometimes Jeffrey would scratch his head over the idiosyncrasies of the Central Vermont audience. He reluctantly acceded to our request to play Ken Loach's Spanish Civil War drama *Land and Freedom*, and was amazed that it did well. Conversely, he aggressively went after Quentin Tarantino's *Pulp Fiction* for us, but the lines down the block did not materialize. I knew we were in trouble when the tenth male customer bought a ticket that opening Friday and said, "I couldn't get my wife to come." The Savoy had always been both a supporter and a beneficiary of Central Vermont's feminist culture; however, the advance word on this film was that, well-made or not, it was crude and brimming with machismo. We may have been the only theater in the country that did not go to the bank on Tarantino's film.[32]

---

[32] A few years later, in 1997, we showed John Sayles' drama *Men With Guns,* set amid a guerrilla war in Central America. After a few days of poor ticket sales, I thought, "If only he had called it *Women Without Guns.*"

CHAPTER 15

A PARTNER IN LIFE AND MOVIES

In March 1999, Gary Ireland's partner, Joanne LaTuchie, received a job offer in Seattle for a prestigious position in her chosen field of housing. Since the opening of the theater in 1981, Gary and I had worked harmoniously, so it was with bittersweet feelings that Gary announced that he and Joanne would be leaving Montpelier. My sadness at saying goodbye to Gary and my uncertain feelings about what lay ahead were tempered by the exciting opportunity for Andrea to become a full partner with me in the ownership of the theater and the video store.

During the previous nine years, Andrea had taken on more responsibility at Downstairs Video. She had been at loose ends in 1990 when the need arose for an assistant manager at Downstairs Video. Andrea's organizational skills made her an ideal fit. In 1991, she became the manager; eight years later, after Gary's departure, we officially became a mom-and-pop business.

Such an arrangement was not uncommon in both of our families. My maternal grandparents, Meyer and Lizzie Kaufman, had operated a dry goods store in the Bronx. One set of Andrea's grandparents, Benjamin and Rose Kohn, also had run a dry goods store, while the other set, Sarah and Abraham Serota, had owned a grocery store (both businesses were in Philadelphia). Andrea's mother, Florence Serota, had been the office manager for Andrea's father Lou's dental practice.

Andrea grew up in Philadelphia and caught the foreign film bug while still in high school. Her senior year French teacher at Girls High had urged the class to see *Children of Paradise,* showing at a nearby movie palace. After watching that extraordinary film, Andrea became a regular at Philadelphia's repertory theaters, an aficionado of Italian films, especially those starring Marcello Mastroianni, and French ones with Alain Delon and Jeanne Moreau. "There was the Bandbox in Germantown, and the World, on Market Street, which showed foreign films in the afternoons," she recalled. "I only afterward guessed it was a porno theater at night."

Moving to New York City to enroll at New York University in 1965, she discovered the riches of the film scene in Greenwich Village. Not only was there the Waverly, the 8th Street Playhouse, the Art, and the Bleecker Street Cinema, but further east there was her favorite, the Village Theater. That movie palace on Second Avenue had a rich history, starting life in 1926 as the Commodore, which presented silent films and vaudeville in both Yiddish and English. It became primarily a movie theater when it was purchased by the Loew's chain, but during the early 1940s also presented live performances of Yiddish plays (broadcast by radio station WLTH). It became the Village Theater in 1963, operating as a venue for films, live music, and Yiddish theater revivals, before beginning its new life as the famed Fillmore East in 1968.

In the summer of 1966, the Village Theater showed a different classic double feature every other night. Andrea remembered well the sweltering heat in the summer of 1966. "I was living in a fifth-floor walkup, and apart from riding the Staten Island Ferry, our only relief was the air-conditioning at the Village Theater. I went there every other night, sometimes every night. I was immersed in a wonderfully random film education." Many of the movies she saw that summer remained her favorites in the years ahead; after we were married, it was a particular satisfaction to revisit them together.

We worked well as a team, due to our mutual love of film and our shared devotion to the Central Vermont community. It was largely thanks to Andrea that Downstairs Video developed into the library/ "cultural speakeasy" that it did. Our trips to New York—when we'd see two or three films a day over a long weekend—were not only stimulating getaways but potentially helpful to the theater. Over Szechuan food on West 72nd Street or Indian food on East 6th Street, we'd discuss what we had just seen and its prospects in Montpelier.

One of the keys to our harmonious working relationship, according to Andrea, was having two separate offices, two floors apart. Referring to her brief experience as an early childhood educator, she termed it "parallel play." She could be as orderly as she wanted in the basement video store, and I could spread out, often chaotically, in the more spacious Savoy office. "How do you ever find anything up here?" she'd ask.

After Gary's departure, we grappled with issues both immediate and long-range, always arriving at a mutually acceptable decision. Although I was the more public face of the Savoy for many years, I always made sure to credit Andrea for her vital role in maintaining the vision and operation of the theater and video store.

That March of 1999 proved to be a demarcation point in the Savoy's history. Andrea was about to become a full partner just as the first Green Mountain Film Festival was concluding its successful debut. In the years to follow, that event left its own indelible mark on Montpelier.

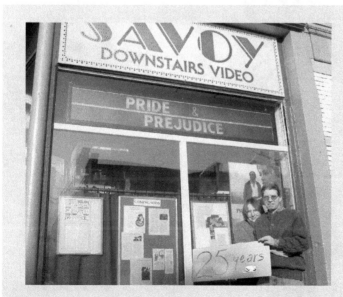

Andrea and I celebrated a milestone in 2006.

2009 Green Mountain Film Festival cover art by John O'Brien.

PART
4

THE GREEN MOUNTAIN FILM FESTIVAL 1999-2012: "A CINEPHILE'S UTOPIA"

CHAPTER 16

A CINEMA VILLAGE ON MAIN STREET 1999–2003

For years I've had a 1982 *New Yorker* cartoon by Mischa Richter taped to the front of a loose-leaf binder. Two cognoscenti are sharing a latte in a café in a tiny village at the top of a steep mountain road, perhaps in Italy. One says to the other, "What this place needs is a film festival." That binder followed me through fourteen iterations of the annual Green Mountain Film Festival.

Unlike the people in the cartoon, I had never been attracted by the idea of putting on a festival in Montpelier. It seemed like a lot of work, a lot of chaos, and I saw no overarching reason to take it on. Andrea and I had enjoyed our trips to the Boston Film Festival and to the Festival du Monde in Montreal, but then our aim was to scout potential features for the Savoy (and to enjoy a big city for a few days). We also loved the thrill of seeing three or four films a day, often not knowing anything about them when we walked in. In Montreal one year, Andrea and I got tickets for a Polish film (*Temptation*) and found ourselves in an audience of about two hundred people—at 9 a.m. on a weekday!—with conversations in Polish going on around us. You couldn't't ask for a more cosmopolitan experience.

Not even such a peak festival-going event, however, convinced us that a festival was something we could—or should—do in Montpelier.

That changed in 1997, when three young and eager film buffs approached the Savoy with the idea of presenting a weeklong festival. They called it the Green Mountain Film Festival. We agreed to be the sponsoring entity and gave them pointers about programming and contacting distributors. Their festival that November was a modest success, but two of the three organizers took jobs elsewhere just after the week ended. After that, Gary and I put the event in the "Oh, well, nice idea" file.

But a year later, in November 1998, our longtime friend and Savoy projectionist Chris Wood asked, "Is anything else ever going to happen with that film festival?" Chris had a life away from the Savoy as a community organizer extraordinaire. He had helped to start the Horn of the Moon Café, the Onion River Arts Council, the advocacy organization Rural Vermont, and the creative Barre hub Studio Place Arts. He was politically active in the antinuclear movement and in protests against our government's involvement in Central America. He also had run a film society at the Plainfield Grange in the early 1980s. So when Chris raised the question of reviving the festival idea, our immediate response was, "If *you* get involved, definitely!!"

Chris Wood in the projection booth.

Suddenly, the thought of putting the Savoy's own stamp on a weeklong celebration of film and film culture became very appealing. Chris took the lead in figuring out how the moving parts would work. Our nonprofit partner Focus on Film, which had been dormant for a few years, sprang back to life as the festival presenter. Jane Knight, who had helped with the 1997 festival, joined us. Two longtime Savoy-goers, Susan Sussman and Dianne Maccario (both board members at Burlington's Vermont International Film Festival), were also excited by the idea and signed on to help with the festival's organization.

How would our very own festival be different from others? Community involvement, for starters. *Best Man,* Ira Wohl's sequel to

Best Boy (Wohl's film about his developmentally delayed cousin), was co-sponsored by the Vermont Coalition for Disability Rights, the Vermont Center for Independent Living, and Beth Jacob Synagogue; *Carla's Song*, Ken Loach's drama set in Nicaragua, was co-sponsored by the Vermont-Nicaragua Construction Brigade; *Delivered Vacant*, Nora Jacobson's documentary on gentrification in Hoboken, New Jersey, was co-sponsored by Central Vermont Community Land Trust and Citizens for Vital Communities.

Focus on Film presents the

Green Mountain Film Festival

March 26–April 1, 1999
Montpelier, Vermont

- 24 Films
- 10 Filmmakers
- Many actors, panels and discussions
- Vermont Premiere of *Mud Season* (filmed in Central Vermont)

SCREENINGS AT:
- Savoy Theater, 26 Main St.
- Pavilion Auditorium, 109 State St

INFORMATION AND TICKETS:
(802) 229-0598

Major funding by Northfield Savings Bank.

The 1999 cover, with a photo by Emily Sloan.

Of the films shown, eight had organizational co-sponsorships, four featured panel discussions, and seven filmmakers came to present their films.

We were ready for a seven-day festival in late March 1999, with twenty-five events, from low-budget, made-in-Vermont features to recently restored classics to American independents. We had scheduled enough films to warrant a second venue: the Pavilion Auditorium, the old home of my Lightning Ridge Film Society. Susan Green, a reporter at the *Burlington Free Press*, quoted me about my experience with that 9 a.m. turnout for the Polish film in Montreal: "We're not at that point yet, but our mission is to ratchet up the interest in film a few more notches." Susan, a longtime film buff herself, could always be relied upon to give the festival a boost each March.

One of the independent films we showed was David Riker's brilliant *La Ciudad*: four short tales, shot in black and white, poignantly depicting the Mexican and Central American immigrant communities in

New York City. Another highlight was the appearance of documentary filmmaker John Cohen, better known to many as one of the founding members of the influential traditional music group, the New Lost City Ramblers.[33] John was also an excellent filmmaker, devoted to the study and appreciation of disparate cultures. He brought a selection of his films, which explored the indigenous Andean population (*Mountain Music of Peru*), the music of Appalachia (*The High Lonesome Sound*), and a Greek community in New York trying to hold on to its traditions (*Pericles in America*).

One film that did not draw a large audience was one of our favorites, Judith Helfand's documentary *A Healthy Baby Girl*. Judith traveled from New York City to talk about her very personal film, in which she explored her mother's decision to take the drug DES during her pregnancy with Judith. This synthetic estrogen, commonly prescribed at the time to prevent miscarriage, was later discovered to have a high cancer risk; it was banned in 1971. The drug had unforeseen and devastating consequences for the entire Helfand family. We lined up several sponsors for this show: the Vermont

A Healthy Baby Girl: "the right twenty people."

Public Interest Research Group, Fletcher Allen Health Care Community Health Improvement Office, and the Governor's Commission on Women. When only twenty people showed up, Andrea and I felt the need to apologize to Judith. She waved us off. "Please don't apologize." In what was to become our own mantra, Judith told us, "If twenty people are here, then they are the right twenty people."

---

[33]The repertoire of the New Lost City Ramblers was largely drawn from 78 rpm records of the 1920s and 1930s. John Cohen, along with other members Mike Seeger, Tom Daley, and Tracy Schwarz, recorded more than twenty-five albums of old-time string band music and early blues starting in 1958, influencing generations of young musicians.

By the end of the seven days, we were all "exhausted and exhila-rated," to quote Andrea. This was going to be a recurring chorus for the remainder of my fourteen years as programming director of GMFF, as we called it. All my previous hesitations about producing a film festival in Montpelier vanished. Instead, I now had the sense that it would be a festival setting, rather than a week-to-week movie house, that had a better chance of promoting our vision of a local film culture. As the 1999 festival came to a close, the question was not "Should we do this again?" but "How can we do it better?"

In our second year, 2000, one aspect of the festival was definitely better. We moved our second venue from the Pavilion Auditorium, a five-minute walk from the Savoy, to right across the street. Montpelier's resident live theater company, Lost Nation Theater, had created an enclosed space (known in the performance world as a "black box") within Montpelier's spacious City Hall Auditorium. Although the logis-tics of projection were always daunting over the next twelve years, this second venue had two hundred seats to the Savoy's 120 and afforded plenty of room for post-film panels and, in time, musical performances. Its proximity to the Savoy also created what Susan Sussman called a "cinema village" on Main Street.

One highlight of the 2000 festival took advantage of City Hall's contours. We sponsored a showing of the rarely seen independent film *Milestones*, directed by John Douglas and Robert Kramer. Their intention was to create—over three hours—a panoramic and immersive study of the state of radical politics in America in the early seventies. One strand of the story was set in Vermont; it involved a rural commune and climaxed in a home birth, captured vividly on film. John Douglas came to speak, as did writer Grace Paley, who had a part in the film, and David Dellinger, one of the notorious "Chicago Seven," who had since settled in Peacham, Vermont. We had a surprise guest as well: Susan Solf, whose home delivery was recorded in the film and whose child was now in her twenties. At the Savoy, having four speakers would have created logistical difficul-ties; the roomy City Hall venue allowed for a relaxed, lively discussion.

Another well-attended festival event took place in 2001, with a surprise hit. *Sound and Fury* was a documentary by Josh Aronson that

John Douglas and Robert Kramer's *Milestones*.

studied an unusual cultural divide: between members of the deaf community and those who opted for the cochlear implant procedure that would restore a better, if somewhat distorted version of their hearing. There were two highly charged discussions—largely carried out in ASL.

The festival was now a well-established and anticipated annual event. And of course, success often brings a need for adaptation. After the 2002 festival, we realized that several changes had to be made. We had had our first two sold-out films (the documentary *The Endurance* and the French film *Code Unknown*, with Juliette Binoche) and knew that if the trend continued, we would have to devise a better ticketing system. The size of the crowds also made us decide to expand to ten days, covering two full weekends, in the following year.

But more urgently, the festival was getting too large to be maintained by an all-volunteer group. Could we afford a managing director? The consensus was that we had to—or else face terminal burnout. Carlos Haase became the festival's first managing director in 2003, followed by Donald Rae in 2006. And so the GMFF entered a new era.

◼ TRAILER:
LA CIUDAD

The trade newspaper *Variety* was an invaluable resource at the Savoy, no matter how off-putting its breezy style ("helmer" was its preferred synonym for "director," and when people left their position at a studio, they "ankled"). For the theater's purposes, we got a sense of what films might be available to us soon and whether they were worth pursu-

David Riker on the set of *La Ciudad.*

ing. For the Green Mountain Film Festival, *Variety* was a must-read because it seemingly had a correspondent at every major and many minor film festivals (though not ours).

While I was programming our first festival in 1999, I noticed an excellent *Variety* review of an independent American film shown at the Sundance Film Festival. The film, *La Ciudad* (The City) was written and directed by a New York University film school graduate, David Riker. Through four discrete stories, *La Ciudad,* shot in black and white for about $500,000, chronicles the experiences of Central American immigrants living in New York City.

The film did not have a distributor yet, but I was able to contact David Riker through the production company, Echo Lake, directly. David not only approved the showing, but accepted our invitation to appear with the film. "I knew next to nothing about where I was headed," recalled David, "but it was enough to know that a print of the film would soon be playing in a darkened room." In one stroke, we had a prestigious film (Roger Ebert had compared it favorably to the Italian neorealist classic *The Bicycle Thieves*) and a visiting filmmaker. David Riker presented his film for two enthusiastic audiences. It gave our small planning group a concrete example of what our own film festival could bring to Montpelier.

A few months later, *La Ciudad* was picked up for distribution by one of our favorite small companies. Zeitgeist Films was attempting to do in the film distribution world what the Savoy was trying to achieve on the exhibition end: defining success in its own modest terms while dealing with the pressures of a hit-obsessed business.

When I was asked to write an article on the film business for *The American Prospect* magazine in 2000, I used *La Cuidad* as my example of the challenges faced by small distributors and exhibitors. I had a chance to interview Nancy Gerstman and Emily Russo, the founders (and longtime co-owners) of Zeitgeist. They had seen Riker's film at the Toronto Film Festival and couldn't believe it was the work of a first-time director. Nancy told me that they couldn't pay David a significant advance, but what they had to offer him was patience, aggressiveness, and a passionate interest. "We could give it our heart and soul," she said.

David Riker invoked one of his filmmaking heroes as he recalled his visit to Montpelier: "As a young filmmaker, I remembered the words of the then-elder statesman of African cinema, Ousmane Sembène, when he was asked why, in his seventies, he was traveling by bus to the most remote villages in Senegal to attend screenings of his newest film, *Guelwaar*. Sembène answered: 'How can I understand what film I have made if I don't see it with the people?'"

TRAILER:
BLACKBOARDS

Hundreds march in Montpelier for peace

By ANNE WALLACE ALLEN
The Associated Press

on the granite steps of the State
House to call for an end to ag.

Thousands march on the
White House, P

"This rush to war has pushed
them over the edge,"

A Montpelier demonstration against the Iraq War.

The winter of 2003 was a time of great anxiety about the world outside of Montpelier. Every weekend, it seemed, there was a protest against the inexorable drive to war against Iraq's ruler, Saddam Hussein. Vermont's U.S. senators, Bernie Sanders and Patrick Leahy, spoke out with little effect against the false "weapons of mass destruction" narrative concocted by President George Bush, Vice President Dick Cheney, Secretary of Defense Donald Rumsfeld, and their minions.

The "shock and awe" bombing marked the beginning of the war in Iraq on March 19, 2003—two days before that year's Green Mountain Film Festival was about to kick off. Our operations committee feared a dismal turnout, assuming that much of our audience would be either glued to TV news or too consumed by helplessness and rage to show up at the movies.

What a surprise, then, to discover our crowds were larger than usual. We soon found out that many moviegoers were disgusted with the jingoistic narrative of the cable news stations (just a month earlier, TV talk show host Phil Donahue had been fired by MSNBC for his antiwar views). Our customers looked to the film festival for a clear-eyed corrective to the inescapable patriotic propaganda—as well as a temporary escape from the news of the day.

No festival film that year captured this moment better than *Blackboards*, an Iranian film set during the Iran-Iraq War of the 1980s. The director was twenty-year-old Samira Makhmalbaf, daughter of two accomplished Iranian film directors. The film follows a pair of itinerant teachers who, blackboards strapped to their backs, wander the desolate mountains of Iran's border with Iraq in hapless search of pupils. One falls in with a group of elderly Iraqi Kurds trying to get back to their bombed village; the other pursues a dozen Kurdish boys who ferry contraband across the border.

When Karen Durbin reviewed the film for the *New York Times* a few months earlier, she said the film "was anything but grim. If Ms. Makhmalbaf is a political filmmaker, she's not a didactic one. Her hallmark is an inexhaustible curiosity. Here, a horrific situation yields pathos, absurdity and humor, as well as something rare: an eye-opening strangeness."

During that turbulent week, audiences did not avoid a film that dealt with the human consequences of Middle Eastern conflict. Instead, they sought it out. The one-sided news from cable television did not allow, as this film did, for a sympathetic treatment of people whose lives were upended by war. With *Blackboards*, the festival amply fulfilled its mandate to show films that mattered.

CHAPTER 17

THE CRITIC'S EYE

Aan event at the 2000 festival had ripple effects through the years that I programmed GMFF. Through a summertime neighbor, the poet Ron Padgett, I had become aware of Rudy Burckhardt, a poet, writer, photographer, and documentary filmmaker. The Swiss-born Burckhardt had emigrated to New York City in 1935 and, starting in the 1940s, began making experimental 16-millimeter films. Burckhardt had died the previous summer, and we invited Ron Padgett to curate a festival tribute to his friend, featuring several of his short films from the 1950s and 1960s. In our festival guide, we quoted the essayist and writer on film, Phillip Lopate: "For the past half-century, Rudy Burckhardt has gone his own way, resisting both the compromises of commercial movie-making and the solemnities of avant-garde cinema."

After the event, Ron suggested that we invite Phillip Lopate himself to attend our next festival, and in 2001, Phillip accepted our invitation. I was jittery about interviewing Phillip, whom I knew by reputation both from my days at Columbia (he had graduated just before my freshman year) and by his voluminous and insightful writings on film. But he quickly put me at ease, talking with great wit and warmth about his own approach to looking at film. "I'm a fifty-year-old white guy," he said. "When I see a film like Baz Luhrmann's *Moulin Rouge!*, I watch it like an anthropologist, pulling back the palm leaves and wondering, what are these young people up to?"

Phillip enjoyed both our conversation and what he saw of the festival. As he was leaving, he generously volunteered to put me in touch with other critics, Stuart Klawans and Molly Haskell among them. So began twelve consecutive years of interviews with a featured film critic at the Green Mountain Film Festival.

I thought about my years as a reader of film criticism as I prepared questions for these discussions. What is the difference between a reviewer and a critic? When you write about a highly anticipated film, how do you try to set aside preconceptions? Do you ever go back and see a film again before writing a review or commentary? Do you ever see films that leave you at a loss about what to say? How do you meet a deadline when that happens? Do you ever go back and change your mind about certain films? How has the corporate takeover of newspapers and the rise of the internet devalued the conversation around film?

Despite being overprepared with these and other questions, I was nervous all over again each year about meeting and interviewing people I knew (and admired) only in print. And each year, I was immediately disarmed by the generosity and the friendliness of our guests. Those who had been to pretentious and glitzy festivals elsewhere were taken with the intimacy of the GMFF.

They were also impressed by the engagement of the Central Vermont audience and the level of their questions: Do you ever watch foreign films without subtitles, if that is the only option? When a film is based on real events, does the critic have an obligation to investigate the truth of its portrayal? Which films do you find most challenging to review? Do you get a certain satisfaction in writing bad reviews?

In my years of subscribing to *The Nation*, I had become an ardent reader of Stuart Klawans' incisive and often wry reviews. Stuart did not show off his erudition by cleverly slamming major Hollywood releases. Instead, he chose to champion smaller films that needed an appreciative audience. He readily accepted our invitation the year after Phillip's visit, and he fell in love with Montpelier. The following year in *The Nation*, he gave us this encomium: "Last year I had the honor of being a guest at the sixth annual Green Mountain Film Festival, held on all two blocks of Montpelier, Vermont. There I discovered a cinephile's utopia: a festival organized and supported by an entire community of local moviegoers. My hosts proved to me that the era of shared enjoyment and discussion is not over."

My conversation with writer David Thomson came about in an unusual way. Andrea and I were at the Montreal World Film Festival in 2005. During a break between films, we wandered toward the McGill University campus, pausing to look at a bookstore window. There was a sign advertising an appearance by David Thomson, talking about the latest edition of his essential reference book *A Biographical Dictionary of Film*. Looking again at the date, we peered through the window to discover that the event was happening at that very moment. We caught the last half-hour of a question-and-answer session. (Responding to a question about film theory, Thomson said, "I just read a ten-page

Interviewing Molly Haskell, 2005.

essay on *The Big Sleep* in a film journal and couldn't understand a word of it!") We approached him afterward and he said he'd be glad to be a festival guest.

Each guest brought a different perspective. Molly Haskell had written the 1974 book *From Reverence to Rape*, a groundbreaking study of the images of women in film, from the early days of silent film to the present. In conversation, she was eloquent on the subject of Hollywood actresses: how female stars were commodified in the studio system, her admiration for rebellious Bette Davis, and the double standard of ageism.

"Why is it that Cary Grant and Harrison Ford can be the romantic hero as they age," she wondered, "while their female counterparts have to be content with playing grandmothers?"

Matthew Hays brought a Canadian view to a discussion of the block-buster syndrome and Hollywood's changing attitudes toward portraying the lives of gays and lesbians. Kathleen Carroll, longtime reviewer for the *New York Daily News*, told of the pressures she encountered when she panned a particular Hollywood film; the New York City offices of the

Godfrey Cheshire's *Moving Midway*.

studio threatened to pull their advertising accounts from the *Daily News* unless she wrote more favorable reviews. Fortunately, these tactics proved to be only show-business bluster.

Critics Godfrey Cheshire and Gerald Peary not only sat for interviews, but each came with a film as well: Godfrey had directed a documentary, *Moving Midway*, about his North Carolina family and their ties to slavery, while Gerry presented his documentary on the history of film criticism, *For the Love of Movies*. Peter Rainer and I had a particularly lively conversation; we were fellow "film nerds" dating back to when we knew each other as teenagers in Westchester County, New York.

I had been an avid listener—every Friday just before 8 a.m.—of National Public Radio's film critic Kenneth Turan, who was also one of the daily reviewers for the *Los Angeles Times*. I was thrilled when he accepted our invitation to appear at the 2011 festival. Along with our interview at Montpelier's Unitarian Church, he also introduced two of his favorite films, Jean Renoir's French classic *The Rules of the Game* and Edgar Ulmer's Yiddish-language film from 1939, *The Light Ahead* (with New Jersey filling in for rural Poland). During the question period of our interview, one audience member made a passing reference to his glamorous Hollywood life. When he stopped laughing, he noted, "It depends on whether you consider driving for an hour and eating takeout sushi in your car to be the epitome of a glamorous Hollywood life." His life as a daily reviewer, he added, was filled with the stress of deadlines, not to mention Los Angeles traffic. "That's why I'm so happy to be in Montpelier."

Interviewing Kenneth Turan, 2010.

CHAPTER 18

COUNTERPOINT: MUSIC AT THE FESTIVAL

The area between the front row and the screen at the Savoy was tiny (six feet deep and fifteen feet wide). For a post-film discussion, we could feature maybe three speakers at the most. However, the spacious environs at City Hall meant that we could have live music to enhance certain films at the GMFF.

We took our first step in this direction when we showed a Norwegian documentary, *Cool and Crazy*, in 2001. This film followed a men's chorus in a small fishing village in northern Norway, and we invited the recently formed Montpelier Gay Men's Chorus to perform after the film. For the documentary *Awake, My Soul* (2006), about the tradition of shape note singing, we had a thirty-member group of local Sacred Harp singers to demonstrate the music, with many audience members joining in.

No one could sit still when the Burlington-based samba band Sambatucada! rocked City Hall after a showing of Mika Kaurismäki's *The Sound of Brazil* (2004). When the film was *Holding Our Own* (2007) about the role of art and music in hospice care, the Hallowell Singers came up from Brattleboro. There were not too many dry eyes as that hospice choir sang "Angels Hovering Around" and "I Bid You Goodnight" after the film.

The festival executed a hat trick of sorts with the film *Paid to Eat Ice Cream* (2002). We invited David Millstone, a Norwich, Vermont–based contra dance caller and filmmaker, to bring his loving documentary portrait of Bob McQuillen, a longtime fixture of the New England contra dance scene. After we showed the film, both David and Bob answered questions. A half-hour later, the audience reconvened at Montpelier's Unitarian Church for an actual contra dance. David, the filmmaker, called the dance and Bob, the film's subject, played the piano, accompanying the flute and fiddle players in his ensemble, Old New England.

Bob McQuillen: *Paid to Eat Ice Cream*, 2002.

Two memorable festival events, in 2008 and 2009, involved Leonard Bernstein and a remarkable coincidence. One of my parents' favorite television shows in the 1950s had been the arts anthology show *Omnibus*, which was produced by television pioneer Robert Saudek and hosted by the urbane British expatriate Alastair Cooke. Among the memorable *Omnibus* shows were five music lectures by a youthful Leonard Bernstein. What were the odds that Robert Saudek's son, Richard Saudek, and Cooke's daughter, Susan Cooke Kittredge, should both live in the same town, just ten minutes from Montpelier?

Richard and Susan eagerly accepted our invitation to be part of the festival. Richard provided us with DVDs of two of the Bernstein lectures, "The Art of Conducting" and "Beethoven's Fifth Symphony."

After one festival screening in 2008 and another the following year, Richard and Susan regaled the audience with their memories of playing backstage at the television studio as children and amusing themselves at the weekly post-show party at the Cooke home, while the adults smoked, drank, and celebrated.

Omnibus: "the score on the floor" was Robert Saudek's idea.

Three popular music events at the GMFF were the silent films accompanied by my old friend Peter Tavalin. Peter brought his Kurzweil keyboard to play the scores that he composed for three classic, early films: D.W. Griffith's melodrama *Way Down East* (1920), Buster Keaton's Civil War–era comedy *The General* (1926), and Harold Lloyd's *Safety Last* (1923). "My keyboard allows me to program sixteen different combinations of the 'orchestra,'" Peter said. "I could do clarinet with pizzicato strings for a silly moment, flute with muted strings for a pastoral moment, or full orchestra with cymbals crashing, timpani rolling, brass blaring, for the battle scene at the end of Keaton's *The General*."

It was Lloyd's *Safety Last* that was most vivid for me. The final nail-biting twenty minutes show Lloyd's death-defying climb up the face of a multistory office building. The sight of Lloyd dangling from a clock face is one of silent film's most iconic images. Peter had composed a virtuoso score for the occasion, as thrilling as what was on the screen. When I asked him about his technique, he replied, "I'm improvising every time I

Safety Last: a thrill a minute.

perform, even the same movie, and draw on all kinds of musical devices to match up with the action or the mood. I can guarantee you I never did the climb the same way twice and have performed *Safety Last* at least thirty times."

In 2011, one of my final years programming the festival, we hosted the sui generis musical virtuoso David Amram. The occasion was a documentary by Larry Kraman called *David Amram: The First 80 Years.* After the showing of the documentary, Amram commandeered the City Hall piano and improvised lyrics for a jazzy tribute to Montpelier and the film festival. He clearly would have kept going all night, but we had another show to usher in. The next morning David and I had our own festival event, a conversation at the Savoy about his film work: he had scored *The Manchurian Candidate* for John Frankenheimer and *Splendor in the Grass* for Elia Kazan before souring on the strictures of Hollywood.

These musical events are among my fondest memories of the festival. Those evenings provided insight, uplift, entertainment, and community, allowing the Green Mountain Film Festival to fulfill its mission many times over.

CHAPTER 19

BEHIND THE SCENES
AT THE FESTIVAL

There were many memorable films and events during my fourteen years as programming director of the Green Mountain Film Festival. So many spring to mind: a visit from the legendary documentary filmmaker Les Blank; poet and NPR commentator Lloyd Schwartz presenting a program on "Music in the Movies"; feature films not only in French or Spanish but in Tagalog (*Crying Ladies*), Chadian Arabic (*Abouna*), Inuktitut (*Before Tomorrow*), and Yolngu Aboriginal dialect (*Ten Canoes*). There were also a number of behind-the-scenes occurrences—some gratifying and some nerve-wracking—that have stayed with me. Here are a few of those.

Burma VJ

When it came time to prepare for the 2010 festival, I became aware of a Danish documentary called *Burma VJ: Reporting from a Closed Country*, whose subtitle accurately described the bravery of the video journalists (the "VJ" of the title) who risked their lives to capture the turmoil of the protests against the military dictatorship in Burma, a.k.a. Myanmar. The reviews were uniformly positive (A.O. Scott of the *New York Times* called it "mesmerizing, with a fascinating mixture of directness and sophistication"), and the distributor, Oscilloscope Pictures, was one of our mainstays.

It was a film that begged for some speaker or panel to augment the experience. But it was not clear how that might come about. I had the idea to consult with my good friend of forty-five years, my college roommate, Alan Senauke. Alan is a Zen Buddhist priest at the Berkeley Zen Center and was formerly the executive director of the Buddhist Peace Fellowship. In 2010, his new organization, the Clear View Project, was very involved with the activities of the Buddhist monks in Burma who were at the heart of the protests.

Alan suggested I call a friend in Brooklyn, who in turn put me in touch with the upstate New York farm where some of the refugee monks were staying. The result was that four Burmese monks, one of whom was featured in the film, arrived in Montpelier, clad in their traditional saffron robes, ready to appear with that evening's showing of *Burma VJ* at City Hall. A full house greeted them with a prolonged ovation. As I reported to Alan later that week, "I have hardly ever felt so much energy and concentration in one room."

With the monks who appeared with *Burma VJ*.

For this event, we had secured two interpreters through the Vermont Refugee Resettlement Program, Htar Htar and Htun Sein. At another showing a few days later, Htun Sein returned, this time as our featured speaker. He told of his own experiences: traveling through the Burmese jungle for a month at age nine, spending four years in a refugee camp on the Thai border, and then connecting with a group that brought him to Vermont.

It was so much more than a night at the movies for all of us. Everyone who was there those nights felt an intensely personal connection to international events outside our Vermont bubble.

Nosey Parker

John O'Brien grew up in Tunbridge, Vermont. It's hard to pin John down: he has been an artist, a sheep farmer, a state representative, and a filmmaker. His delightful low-budget feature *Vermont Is For Lovers* did well at the Savoy in 1992, but that modest success paled in comparison to his next feature, in 1996. It was then that he cast his farmer neighbor Fred Tuttle as an unlikely candidate for the U.S. Senate in *Man With a Plan*. That film, fueled by its tagline "Spread Fred," became a Vermont phenomenon and led to Fred's candidacy in an actual Senate campaign in 1998.

Of course, we eagerly (and patiently) awaited John's next venture, seven years later. It was another low-key slice of small-town Vermont life, titled *Nosey Parker*. John readily agreed to a two-showing spotlight at the 2003 GMFF, anticipating a regular run at the Savoy after the festival.

The theater was packed for that first show, at 9:30 on a Saturday morning. The film had been underway for twenty minutes when the projectionist, Chris Wood, noticed something ominous: smoke filling the projection booth. What we learned later was that our maintenance procedure for the projectors, which included checking and changing the oil, had either been ignored or had gone awry ("I thought she/he was going to do it!").

Assigning responsibility was not a priority at that moment. The motor on that projector had clearly burned out. Chris quickly shut the

Man With a Plan: Filmmaker John O'Brien and his star actor, Fred Tuttle.

machine down, and as I went to the front of the theater and begged for the audience's patience, Chris transferred the reel in progress to the other projector. That saved the immediate show, but we had five more shows that day and then six the next. We couldn't run them all on one projector without the risk of burning out that projector's bulb (the high-powered xenon bulbs in our projectors—not easily replaced— worked most efficiently with cooling intervals).

What followed convinced us that the cinema gods were smiling on the Green Mountain Film Festival that day. I frantically called our projector technician Bill Templeman, who lived in the Boston area. He happened to be home and answering his phone on a Saturday morning. "First of all," Bill said, "get every fan you can find, turn them all on high and direct the breeze at the working projector." He then suggested we call his friend in Maine who dealt in used projector parts. That person, too, happened to be home and answering his phone. And yes, he had a replacement motor for a Simplex machine.

That was the good news. The bad news was that the motor was in Maine and it was already eleven o'clock in the morning, with another show coming in at noon. Susan Sussman, a GMFF board member, had a brilliant idea. She discovered a car service, not too far from where our motor was waiting, and arranged for the pickup and delivery to Montpelier. The motor wouldn't get to the Savoy until six, but we could make it until then.

That solved one problem, but what was going to happen once the replacement motor arrived at the theater? No one on our staff had the deep technical expertise to install such a vital part. But once again, Bill Templeman was ready to help via telephone. He acted as air traffic controller, talking Andrew Kline, Chris Wood, and Carlos Haase through the whole process step by step. The booth, with six fans going and three projectionists on hand, had never been such an intensely concentrated crucible.

No one in the audience could tell when the newly repaired projector was back in use at half-past eight that evening. But there were cheers and high-fives all around the booth and the lobby. Once the adrenaline wore off, we all slept quite well that night.

Albert Maysles

One day in the summer of 2007, Andrea and I had lunch with our friend Charlotte Potok, a longtime Plainfield resident and an imaginative, prolific potter. She suggested that we invite her old friend Albert Maysles to the festival. "Albert Maysles!" we exclaimed. "You know Albert Maysles?" To documentary watchers the world over, the name Maysles casts a magic spell. Together with his brother David, Albert had revolutionized the world of intimate, cinema vérité filmmaking, with

The legendary documentarian Albert Maysles.

such classics as *Salesman* (a 1968 film that followed a door-to-door Bible salesman) and *Grey Gardens* from 1975 (a disturbing portrait of aristocrats gone to seed, Edith Bouvier Beale and her daughter, also named Edith, a.k.a. "Little Edie").

"Oh, yes, I know him," Charlotte said. In fact, Albert had been her boyfriend in the late 1940s. Charlotte saw Vermont for the first time when she and Albert had hitchhiked here. At the time, Albert was studying psychology, but as a result of working on a documentary about psychiatry in the Soviet Union in 1955, he became a filmmaker. "Be sure to mention my name," Charlotte told us.

With that entrée, Albert Maysles traveled from New York City to be a guest of honor at the 2008 Green Mountain Film Festival. Albert was then eighty-two, and we had very special instructions from our contact at Maysles Films: we should find someone to be a "minder"—that is, to accompany him to meals and to the venue, and to make sure he had his afternoon nap. Oh, yes, and we should make sure he had a bottle of his favorite vodka on hand at the inn.

Our friend Dave Raizman, who had just started a videography business in Montpelier, readily agreed to help us out. We had scheduled a busy day for Albert: *Salesman* at 1:00, *Grey Gardens* at 4:00, and *Gimme Shelter* (about the Rolling Stones at the ill-fated Altamont Festival) at 8:00, all with question-and-answer sessions. I had assumed, given that these films were thirty to forty years old, that their creator had seen them many times and would be using the screenings as a time to rest. But no . . . Albert turned out to be an energetic octogenarian who wanted to have the experience—once more—of seeing how an audience reacted to his films. The discussions were lively, and the enthusiastic crowd charged his batteries.

Dave Raizman fondly recalled Albert Maysles's love of Montpelier's downtown and Albert's curiosity about everyone he met that weekend. "In Zen practice, they call it 'beginner's mind,'" Dave said. "For someone so accomplished and esteemed, he had no sense of self-importance." Dave asked Albert if he had any advice about video camera work. "Just hold it steady," was Albert's response.

There was a bittersweet postscript to this memorable day. By the time the festival was underway, Charlotte Potok was dying of cancer. The day after those three film showings, Dave drove Albert to Plainfield, where Albert spent one last afternoon with his old friend. Charlotte died that summer. Before Albert Maysles died several years later, at age eighty-eight, he had directed five more documentaries.

The Visitor

In January 2008, I saw an excellent review in *Variety* for an as-yet-unreleased film called *The Visitor*. The writer-director was Tom McCarthy, whose previous film was the sensitive *The Station Agent*. The new one was described by *Variety* as a "soulful and humanistic post-9/11 drama" that starred the longtime supporting actor Richard Jenkins, who finally had a lead role. Jenkins portrayed a college professor whose life is upended when he finds two refugees—one Syrian and one Senegalese—camped in his New York apartment.

The film was one of the first releases of a new distributor, Overture Films. To my delight, they readily agreed to a festival booking, with the understanding that we would bring the film back to the Savoy for a week-long run after it opened in April.

I gathered Overture's promotional material and highlighted the film in our publicity. I was hoping to get the film a few days early, as we did for most other films, and show it to several local journalists. The staff at Overture kept putting me off about when it would arrive, and the hectic days before the festival meant that we'd be lucky to preview the film ourselves.

I was getting frantic as our Friday opening night loomed. Our first showing of *The Visitor* was scheduled for Saturday afternoon at 2:00, and it was already sold out. When I was finally able to reach someone in the Overture office, I was assured that *The Visitor* would arrive via Fed Ex on Friday afternoon. But there was a catch: the film was going to arrive with its "Goldbergs" (the octagonal shipping cans) locked. They would be opened in person on Saturday morning by someone Overture had hired—a "rent-a-cop" who would drive over from Plattsburgh, New York—to make sure that the film was not pirated before it opened nationally.

That was only the beginning of Overture's precautions, as we found out the day of the show. The person Overture hired (I'll call him Frank) arrived an hour before the film was scheduled to be shown, so the projectionist quickly got to work at the splicing table once the film can locks were undone. Now Frank delivered the rest of Overture's demands: we had to collect everyone's cell phone as they entered the theater! Frank would also patrol the aisles every fifteen minutes with night vision goggles to make sure there was no piracy hanky-panky.

We couldn't believe this was happening! A number of us took turns explaining to Frank what irrational and difficult-to-enforce demands

Overture was making. He listened sympathetically but raised his hands in a "I'm only the messenger" gesture.

While this scene was unfolding in the lobby a half-hour before showtime, one of our most resourceful volunteers, Andrea Stander, was upstairs in the ticket office, working on the cell phone problem. She devised an elaborate system of keeping track of everyone's phone so the phones could be retrieved easily and returned to the right owners when the show was done.

But by the time Andrea came downstairs with her system, the festival had worked its magic. Our lead volunteer that day, Alison Underhill, made it her project to make Frank feel welcome. She explained to him the nature of the community event he had happened into, giving him a brief history of the festival and its place in Montpelier. Piracy would be the last thing on anyone's mind. "No one in this audience would do such a thing," she told him. "They are only here to enjoy the film . . . and what's more, you're welcome to join them."

Just as the line of ticket holders outside was about to come in, Frank relented. In a voice barely above a whisper, he said, "If you won't tell, I won't tell." Of course he had to guard our print of *The Visitor* until we were done with it the next day. But by then, he had made some friends, enjoyed some popcorn, watched some good films, and learned firsthand about the warmth of our movie-loving town. He even let some of the staff try out his night vision goggles. I'd like to think he was sad to leave us on Sunday.

Harvard Beats Yale, 29-29

That was the headline in the *Harvard Crimson* after a historic football game in 1968, in which Harvard came back from what seemed to be a sure loss to tie the game in the final seconds. It also served as the enigmatic and humorous title for a unique 2008 documentary.

The film opened in November 2008, with the *New York Times*'s Manohla Dargis calling it "preposterously entertaining." It was perfect timing for our 2009 festival in March. Another plus: the film would give some balance to a lineup already weighted with serious documentaries. We were also going to be showing *At the Death House Door*, about prison

Harvard Beats Yale, 29-29.

chaplain Carroll Pickett; *The Brother*, about David Greenglass, whose testimony sent his sister Ethel Rosenberg to the electric chair in 1953; *The Singing Revolution*, which documented the Estonian uprising of 1991; and *Torturing Democracy*, an exposé of the Central Intelligence Agency's enhanced interrogation techniques.

Although the Harvard-Yale film seemed like a sure bet to be included in the festival, I wanted to screen it just to make sure (and, of course, I couldn't wait to see it). An opportunity to preview the film came one slow night at Downstairs Video. I put the DVD in the machine and was immediately taken with the humor and the scope of the film. Although the subject was one particular football game, that game was played at a tumultuous historic moment: the Vietnam War was raging, and many college campuses were in turmoil. As the filmmaker Kevin Rafferty and the interview subjects (players on both teams) made clear, the game was not played in a vacuum.

At one point I was helping a video customer and missed a few minutes of the action. I could still hear the soundtrack, and I was sure I heard a familiar voice coming from the television. Now who did that remind me of? After the customer left, I skipped back to see the identification of that one ex-football player whose voice had registered: Bill Kelly, a Harvard quarterback, who had a small but crucial part in Harvard's "victory." Of course! Bill had exactly the same measured delivery and intonation as my Plainfield friend Tom Kelly. Could they be brothers? A quick phone call cleared up any doubt.

That's how Bill Kelly came to be a guest at our showing in March. He initially had to be persuaded to appear with the film. He had never seen it and was self-conscious about seeing himself on screen. But once he was in Montpelier and sat through the sold-out screening, he realized that the film was more than a straight-ahead documentary. "I was blown away," he recalled. "I was amazed that one afternoon in 1968 could provide so much entertainment and social commentary forty years later."

Bill regaled the crowd with stories that hadn't made it into the film, especially how the sense of "cosmic inevitability" took over the entire Harvard team as the clock ticked down. No one enjoyed the film more than Bill's teenage daughter Jessie. She was beaming with pride as she watched the film and saw her father revealed as a hero.

Butterfly

One crucial set of volunteers at the Green Mountain Film Festival was the screening committee. Most of the films selected for the festival were there as a result of my own in-depth reading of newspapers like the *New York Times*, trade periodicals like *Variety*, and specialized journals like *Film Comment*. Other films might arrive unsolicited in the mail from independent filmmakers who had heard about our festival.

For a few films—such as a restored classic from the 1950s or an as-yet-unreleased film from a major director—I was quite willing to make the decision myself. But usually I felt it was important that other supporters of the festival's goals should be included in the process. Perhaps my enthusiasm for a particular film wasn't shared by anyone else, or a film that sounded good on paper left our screeners cold. Maybe the ten local film buffs who composed the screening committee had ideas for panels and sponsorship (a crucial part of our programming) that I hadn't thought of.

Film distributors, eager to have a booking, would send us VHS tapes, then DVDs as that technology became more common. I devised a sign-out process so that committee members could preview the film, and I included a questionnaire for them to fill out. One question asked for suggestions about groups that might be likely "community partners," as we called them: organizations that would help get the word out to their own membership. But there was another question that led to some controversial program choices: "Do you think the festival should show this film, even if you didn't like it?"

The festival's first episode showing one of these "I didn't like it, but ..." films was a memorable one: *Butterfly*, a documentary about the environmental heroine and tree sitter Julia "Butterfly" Hill. Hill gained the attention of the world for her two-year vigil living on a small platform 180 feet atop what she called an "ancient" redwood tree, preventing it from being toppled by a logging company. Doug Wolens directed the film for Public Television's *POV* (filmmaking shorthand for "point of view") series. It aired in June 2000 and became available to play at our 2001 festival.

It seemed like an easy decision: a film about one person's challenge to environmental destruction would certainly draw an audience in Central Vermont. But I thought it would be wise to get some opinions from our screening committee.

The reviews had been mostly positive, though the *New York Times* critic Lawrence Van Gelder raised questions that foretold some strong reactions by our screeners: "Is she spiritual kin to Gandhi? Brave sister to Rosa Parks? Or is she simply a rebellious, self-righteous post-adolescent reveling in an outpouring of attention?"

Our screeners apparently agreed with Van Gelder's third option: everyone on the committee hated the film—or, more accurately, its protagonist. One screener said, "By the end of the film, I wanted to strangle her." But the unanimous verdict was yes, we should show it. We agreed that it was a well-made documentary, that there was bound to be interest in the subject, and that we might anticipate some spirited discussion about Hill's motivation.

The decision to show the film was a good one. With support from a local environmental group, Forest Watch, the festival hosted two sold-out screenings of *Butterfly*, with not a trace of the negative reaction of our screeners. For years to come, members of the screening committee would ask, "OK, what's going to be our *Butterfly* film this year?"

CHAPTER 20

A CINEMA VILLAGE ON MAIN STREET, PART TWO: 2004-2012

During the fourteen years I programmed the Green Mountain Film Festival, the event offered satisfactions that the operation of the Savoy could not. First, there was the financial aspect. A nonprofit organization responsible for producing a ten-day event did not face the week-to-week pressures that were a fact of life for the theater: no payroll to meet, suppliers to pay, overhead to cover. The GMFF had sponsors who could, and did, underwrite the costs of the festival, often with enthusiasm.

A second element was the content of the festival. Whether the films we selected were documentaries, independent or international features, or restorations of older classics, what they had in common was that they would not do well for an entire weeklong run at the Savoy. Three showings of the Norwegian comedy *Kitchen Stories*, for example, drew an audience of three hundred with just three shows—probably twice the attendance had it played as a regular feature for a week.

Finally, there was the collaborative nature of the festival, which manifested in several ways. Working with the twelve-member ops committee, as it came to be known, was a highlight for me each year, a chance to work together with others dedicated to a common goal. With good humor and team spirit, the "ops" addressed the inevitable challenges that arose with the growth of the festival.

Beyond the ops committee, there were the festival volunteers—sometimes as many as fifty. Some were behind the scenes, helping out at the ticket office or previewing films for our screening committee. Some were quite visible, enabling one audience to completely file out of the theater before the next filed in. Some picked up our guests at the Burlington airport, and some helped organize our "Goldberg" film cans for delivery when the show was over.

In all, the festival felt like a true community phenomenon in a way that the Savoy could never be. The Savoy, despite its status as an outlier in the world of commerce, was still a business with a day-to-day operation. The festival created a sense that everyone—sponsors, volunteers, and attendees—was, for ten days, participating in an explosion of film culture in Montpelier.

One year, a festival attendee stopped me and said excitedly, "That was the first time I've ever seen two movies in one day!" Others, who had experience watching double features, now upped their intake to three, even four in one day. I came to a new understanding of all that the term "film culture" implied as I saw it blossom right in front of me. I started to hear stories of strangers striking up conversations—whether in line outside, in their theater seats, or at restaurants afterward—about the movies they had seen. Recommendations were made, and occasionally, so I heard, phone numbers were exchanged.

The festival had its own cycle, apart from that of the Savoy. During the Savoy's history, there were years when we were a "calendar house"—that is, there were set dates for the run of a film. Other times we gave ourselves flexibility to hold a film over. But in either case, we mailed a newsletter every five or six weeks, with descriptions of what would or might be coming soon. No sooner did a flyer go into the mail than the planning began for the next round.

But the addition of the festival as a major annual event set up another cycle. To plan a festival that was held each March, our all-volunteer operations committee met for the first time in September, a full six months beforehand.

Was the festival going to be different in any way next March? Were there going to be added expenses? Were there possibilities for new major sponsors? (Or, more critically, were any major sponsors dropping out?) How were we going to change our ever-evolving ticketing method? Could we add a new venue? Were there any themes—immigration, race, the environment—emerging as the films were selected? What panels might bring a local perspective on issues?

Lines like this were common each March.

As programming director, I was constantly on the lookout for films that would be ideal for the festival: documentaries that might prove a good fit for sponsorships or panel discussions, restorations of old classics, and feature films that might have a limited audience if they ran for a full week at the Savoy instead of two showings at the festival. The conversations continued at home as Andrea and I speculated over breakfast about who might be the next featured critic or how we could make the festival an even more enriching experience for everyone.

A challenge we faced every year was to find a good comedy to provide some balance to the mainly serious fare we showed. Major filmmakers the world over—not just documentarians—were drawn to weighty topics like immigration (Jean-Pierre and Luc Dardenne's *Lorna's Silence*), bigotry (Ken Loach's *Sweet Sixteen*), and social inequality (Sebastian Silva's *The Maid*). Despite some popular conceptions to the contrary, we really were trying to find some lighter films to balance our program. Two memorable discoveries were the German/Turkish road movie *In July* and the French romantic comedy *Avenue Montaigne*.

By January each year, most of the films were selected. I began to write the copy for the program and to gather promotional material. But the actual scheduling was the result of several factors. How many times a film might be shown was often limited contractually. In many cases, the film's venue was determined by its format: 35-millimeter (definitely the Savoy), 16-millimeter (usually City Hall), VHS or later DVD (definitely at City Hall).

To map out the ten-day schedule, we set up a template on two large pieces of illustration board, one for the Savoy and one for City Hall. Each space on the grid was sized to fit one Post-it note, with the film title and running time. Was there a family film that might be appropriate for a weekend daytime slot? Was there enough time to add a late show, and was there a film appropriate for one? How much time should we allot for a panel discussion? Should a film play two or three times? And trickiest of all, how could we arrange the timing so moviegoers could go back and forth across the street without missing the beginning of a film?

These scheduling sessions were full of camaraderie and excitement as we watched the approaching festival take shape on the two boards. Inevitably a cheer would go up when the last spot was filled in. Now that we had the times and the venues, it was on to the next big task: putting together the physical program guide. This involved proofreading before handing the dates and descriptions over to a graphic artist—Brian Prendergast, Linda Mirabile, or other talented local designers—and then another few rounds of proofreading when the draft was ready.

Then came the task of arranging, scheduling, and sitting down for interviews with radio stations and newspapers. My favorite spot was WGDR, the Goddard College radio station, where each year host Joseph Gainza gave me a full hour to discuss the festival offerings. Susan Green at the *Burlington Free Press*, Margot Harrison at *Seven Days*, and a rotating staff at our local *Times Argus* were all eager to publicize the festival.

In the meantime, there were funds to raise, panel discussions to arrange, volunteers to recruit, a ticket office to make functional. Then there were the flyers to mail and distribute, and the projection booth

The festival's City Hall venue.

traffic to organize. Often the films were on "the festival circuit" and were shipped to us from film festivals in other cities; in turn, we had to ensure that the films went on their way speedily to their next venue. Occasionally, the time constraints turned into nail-biters; in 2000, I had to go to the Burlington airport to pick up our opening night film, the Cuban drama *Life Is to Whistle*, and returned to Montpelier with just a half-hour to spare before the curtain went up.

There was so much preparation and attention to detail that we organizers were usually exhausted by the time the festival began. At the Savoy it often felt we were giving a party and five hundred people showed up at once. It was at times overwhelming, but the immediate feedback from a gratified audience gave us all the adrenaline we needed to make it to the finish line.

Our late friend Cora Brooks told us that she loved the festival because she could go around the world without leaving Montpelier. Another regular attendee, Jane Edwards, said she loved the festival because of its timing for the last two weeks of March: "When you go in, it's winter and when you come out, it's spring." Nora Lovelette, an experienced festival volunteer, recalled, "You knew it was festival time when you could smell the popcorn through the mud." We heard from several attendees that they took their allotted time off work during those ten days to see twenty and sometimes thirty films.

After a day of cleanup, our ops committee would gather for a celebratory dinner. On one occasion, after a Chinese feast at The Single Pebble restaurant in Berlin, Andrea and I returned to the theater on our way home. I've long since forgotten what our particular errand was, but there, slipped under the door, was an envelope. It held a cashier's check for $8,000 with an unsigned note saying, "Thank you for doing what you do."

Over the years, the festival organization experienced growing pains familiar to many in the nonprofit world. The constant concern for festival organizers was growth. How much and how quickly? With each incremental enhancement of the festival, we feared that it would lose the intimate character that so many moviegoers valued. We also became very aware of the various hidden cleaning and maintenance costs after the wear and tear of a ten-day stampede. The ever-changing relationship between the festival and the Savoy also became a constant dynamic. For the first few years of the festival, the Savoy cut the festival a lot of slack, but by 2006, the festival's growth coincided with a gradual decline in the Savoy's yearly attendance. Now it was the theater that came to depend on the income of the festival.

After many banner years for the festival, my involvement ended abruptly after the 2012 festival. I have since learned that the scenario is a familiar one in the nonprofit world: differing visions about the festival's future led to a fracturing conflict on the board. I was not exactly fired, but a board implosion created an untenable situation.[34] This was a difficult time for me, but I will always cherish my years helping make the Green Mountain Film Festival "a cinephile's utopia."

---

[34]The festival continued for several years after I left. The Covid-19 pandemic temporarily halted the festival, but there are plans to resume in 2024.

Savoy 15th anniversary cartoon by Tim Newcomb.

PART 5

THE SAVOY 2000-2009: "THE LONG GOODBYE"

CHAPTER 21

TAKING CARE OF BUSINESS

Some people may have romantic notions of operating a movie theater. Perhaps it has to do with childhood associations of sitting in the darkness and being mesmerized by larger-than-life, often colorful images. Perhaps it has to do with the glamour of whatever exotic settings or vivid personalities are onscreen. Perhaps they were charmed by the sentimental Italian film *Cinema Paradiso*, in which a young boy forms an attachment to a crusty but lovable old movie projectionist.

But whenever I mentioned to friends that I was working at the theater that morning, quite a few seemed surprised. What could possibly keep me occupied in the mornings? Isn't running a theater just a matter of hanging out until evening, then turning on the lights, projector, and popcorn machine and waiting for the crowds to arrive?

To demystify the behind-the-scenes life of the theater, here are a few typical days, starting with a busy Monday. The first task on Monday mornings was to study the weekend receipts to determine whether the film did well enough to warrant another week (this was after we went "off calendar" to give ourselves some flexibility in holding popular films).[35] Our *Times Argus* ad rep arrived around 11:00 a.m. to find out which ads we'd be running and when. The paper needed that information right away in order to place an announcement on Thursday about "ends tonight" and "starts tomorrow."

After a weekend, we had to check our concession supplies. A busy Friday through Sunday might mean that we had to order fruit juice, high-oleic oil for the popcorn machine, more fifty-pound bags of popcorn, and of course the Savoy concession standby, nutritional yeast. It is impossible to say how many customers over the years got hooked on augmenting their popcorn with that yellow powder, which—especially when combined with butter—makes a tub of popcorn undergo an almost magical, nutty-flavored transformation. (Although many people credit the Savoy with introducing nutritional yeast as a popcorn addition, the idea was not ours originally; the Playhouse Theater in nearby Randolph got there first.)

After the concession check, Gary and I (and, after Gary's departure, Andrea and I) would look at the staffing schedule for the week. Were there holes to fill? Might someone have failed in their efforts to find a sub? Then there was a meeting with our bookkeeper to discuss both our current balance and looming expenses. After the payroll was done, did we have any wiggle room to pay our suppliers, both local (popcorn and popcorn cups, paper towels, cleaning supplies, advertising, etc.) and in the film distribution world? If we were not up to date on our payment for *Little Miss Sunshine*, then perhaps we were at risk of losing the next film from that film's distributor, Fox Searchlight.

Wednesday was the day to find out whether there were going to be any shipping problems with the Friday film. If all went well, the "Goldbergs" containing the film would be waiting in the lobby on Friday morning. Then one of us on the staff would splice the film together and preview it, making sure it came to us in good shape. I remember one morning when it was my task to splice *Music Box*, a film starring Jessica

---

[35]For years, we had been a "calendar house," meaning that our flyer had fixed dates and times for every show. Though patrons living miles from the Savoy could count on a certain film playing at a definite time, one major downside to this system was not being able to take advantage of an unexpected success by holding it for another week, or perhaps longer. Our booker, Jeffrey Jacobs, convinced us that we should take the leap to go "off calendar" and find new ways to keep our audience informed of our schedule.

Lange. It didn't take much of an inspection to realize that whichever theater had it before us had sent it on in sorry shape. The film would never have made it through the projector without breaking at several points. It took me about two hours to piece together one five-minute section of the film.[36]

Putting together a film on a Friday morning.

Each morning there was a trip to the Northfield Savings Bank. The previous night's take had been deposited after closing; now it was time to pick up the deposit slips and replenish our change supply. On any day of the week, there might be a meeting with an electrician or plumber or projector repair person to fix a problem. Or a meeting with a new supplier demonstrating their wares. Or a meeting with our friends at

---

[36]Though neither of us was mechanically inclined, Gary and I had wisely decided to learn the basics of booth mechanics so we could step in when needed. We had two superb teachers: our original Savoy projectionists, Norman Bloom and Andrew Kline.

the nearby restaurant with whom we were exploring a dinner-plus-movie combination.

Every once in a while we had a personnel problem to discuss. An employee whom we liked showed up late or missed shifts. How should we handle that? Another employee was returning to school come September and needed to be permanently replaced. There was a potential hit film coming up; should we double up on the concession stand? Which former concession staffers were now home from college and able to give us a hand?

For many years, two very gifted graphic designers—first Tim Newcomb and then Brian Prendergast—rented the rear section of our office.[37] Thanks to their generosity and patience, I became conversant in the PageMaker and InDesign programs and was ready to design my own calendar layout. On some mornings, I'd be working on the layout, writing the descriptions of coming films and choosing the most eye-catching graphics. The next step was bringing the layout sheets to the printer (it was a big day when we could finally do this step via email).

When the calendar was ready, there was the grunt work of printing the address labels, slapping them on each flyer, and organizing the bulk mailing that went out to more than two thousand patrons on our mailing list. To this day, I can tell you that Johnson, Vermont is 05656, while Winooski is 05404. Periodically the post office would issue new guidelines and we'd have to reorient ourselves about which stickers to affix and which canvas bag got which zip code.

In my spare office moments, I would pore over *Variety* or *Box Office* or *Film Journal* to see what might be ahead. Which films should we consider for Christmas or the summer? Or, putting on my film festival hat, which films sounded promising, although for a specialized audience? Which posters and other ad material should we order?

As I remarked to a friend, it was a forty-hour week but far from a nine-to-five routine. The hours were spread through the week in an odd

---

[37]While Tim shared our office, we'd take our lunch breaks every Tuesday across the hall at Haskell Pottery. In between bites, we'd play music: me on accordion, Tim on fiddle, Paul Haskell on guitar, and Jeanne Haskell on concertina. It was music therapy for all of us!

This is where it all happened: my desk in the Savoy office.

fashion, often changing from week to week. When many people looked forward to Friday and a respite from work, the weekend was just when it all started for me.

The importance of a flexible workday came home to me when an opportunity arose to open a branch of the Savoy in Burlington. We were approached by someone who had bought a building downtown, just the right size for a Savoy-on-the-Champlain. What did we think? We didn't have to think for very long. The combination of raising the necessary funds, facing heavier competition in that urban environment, working longer hours, and commuting two hours a day between the two sites made it an easy decision: No! Just thinking about the possibility made me want to take a nap.

As a matter of fact, napping did play a part in the decision. I had managed to order my life so that I had a full afternoon at home between mornings in the theater office and evenings at the concession stand. I could ski, read, garden—or nap. Despite the capitalist imperative to keep expanding whatever the cost—financial or otherwise—I could not see surrendering that freedom. (In Burlington, pioneering entrepreneurs Ben Cohen and Jerry Greenfield—founders of Ben & Jerry's Ice Cream in 1978—had no such reservations about expanding, within Vermont and far beyond.) Gary and I also realized that even though our audiences might be larger, we wouldn't know nearly as many of them. Exchanging news with friends over the concession counter or video desk was a large part of the satisfaction of being at work. And even if we didn't know all our regulars by name, there was gratification in seeing familiar faces week after week.

Savoy fans in Burlington were disappointed but understood our desire to stay put. The Savoy had become an example of what sociologists refer to as "the third space," the place other than home or work that can serve as an anchor for interaction and community life. And we wanted to keep it that way.

TRAILER:
MR. MAGOO FINDS HIS SEAT

Sometime in the early 1990s, it became apparent that our theater seats, purchased secondhand in 1980, were in desperate need of replacement. Hussey Seating, in Berwick, Maine, specialized in theater chairs, for intimate places like ours as well as for plush multiplexes and spacious arenas. The price was roughly a hundred dollars per new seat. Replacing all 125 was going to stretch our meager finances considerably.

Andrea then remembered the fundraisers at the synagogue of her youth and the personalized plaques that adorned the seats. Perhaps we could do something similar at the theater, with our customers paying $100 to endow a seat.

As in our membership campaign of 1986, the response was immediately heartening. Within a week, we had enough pledges to pay for new seats for the entire theater (which are still in use as of this writing).

Some people chose to memorialize friends and family members who died much too soon. Some, like Andrea and me, paid tribute to departed parents.[38] Others memorialized their favorite figures from the film world: the Italian director Michelangelo Antonioni, the cult director Ed Wood Jr., Asta (the fox terrier from *The Thin Man*), Rick and Ilsa from *Casablanca*. There were two in honor of Baptiste, the lovelorn mime of *Children of Paradise*.

A seat honoring the artist and herbalist Adele Dawson.

---

[38]The plaque for my mother Julia was an adaptation of lines from a Shakespeare sonnet: "In thine eyes I read such art as truth and beauty shall forever thrive."

There were also tributes to greatly missed figures in our Central Vermont community. Someone commented that reading the plaques was like embarking on a walking tour of the 1970s.There were plaques honoring the antipoverty crusader Ben Collins; the artist and herbalist Adele Dawson; the former Works Project Administration (WPA) painter and art instructor Ron Slayton; the filmmaker and painter G. Roy Levin; the journalist Stephen Ward; and the creative, free-spirited fixture of the Maple Corner community, Elizabeth Kent Gay.

Some plaques made us laugh out loud. The novelist Annie Proulx, then living in Vermont, requested a plaque "and it has to be in the front row!" No, she was not being difficult. She wanted to honor the nearsighted animation protagonist, Mr. Magoo. On the other end of that continuum, the attorney Scott Skinner asked for a plaque in the seat that was farthest from the screen. He wanted to memorialize the eagle-eyed Red Sox slugger, Ted Williams.

Perhaps my favorite was from friends at Bear Pond Books, just down Main Street. After owner Michael Katzenberg bought a plaque for the bookstore, the staff chipped in for their very own in the next seat over: "The book was better."

TRAILER: "I WAS A TEENAGE POPCORN SCOOPER"

"Brewer's yeast in the middle, please!" was a frequent request.

One of the delights of our workplace was our staff—the projectionists, concessionaires, video clerks, and custodians—who, with their enthusiasm and devotion, were the other public faces of the Savoy. Among these, we took special pleasure in getting to know the teenagers who worked for us over the years. For many of these young folks, working at the theater was their first job. Later, during their college vacations, they would fill in when needed, and after graduation and into adulthood many of them stayed in touch. Here are some of their memories of working at the Savoy:

Sophie Miles: "As a high school student, I loved working with adults and hearing about their lives as parents, barbers, bakers, printmakers, lawyers, photographers, teachers, radio DJs, etc., etc., etc.! This kind of reciprocal contact with grownups was an absolute tonic after leaving eighth period gym class at Montpelier High School. Sometimes the time spent behind the counter with the projectionist (and occasionally another concession staff person) felt like a very short, stationary road trip—a natural container for conversation, inside jokes, and people-watching through the windows. When I worked at the Savoy, this is what I looked forward to, and looking back, it's what I miss most. My time there gave me a quick-reference gut-feeling index of what community feels like when it's real."

Alexander Barrett: "On any evening, when you pushed open the door on your way to pick out a VHS tape, you'd be greeted with a faceful of the smell of popcorn popping and Cabot butter—the good stuff—melting away on a hot plate behind the tiny concession stand/ticket booth. If a film was about to start, you'd weave your way past the line and turn left into the stairway featuring a sign for both Downstairs Video and the theater's bathrooms. You'd dodge patrons running up the stairs from the bathroom, excited to discover the seats their partners claimed for them. One more turn to the left and you'd see it: an oasis of capital-F Film. Handmade wooden shelves lining exposed brick walls, a dense Russian sci-fi film playing on the thirteen-inch TV surrounded by rows and rows of black clamshell VHS boxes arranged in alphabetical order with their spines facing out so the staff could see their handwritten titles, a random sampling of central Vermont's literati perusing the shelves organized by country, not genre, obviously.

For most of my high school years, I got to work down there. I spent every Friday night and Saturday and Sunday afternoon behind the video counter and I loved every second of it. It was where I could truly feel like myself around other people. It's where I could tentatively emerge from my little cocoon and introduce myself to the world."

Sasha Ross Becker: "My job at the Savoy Theater in Montpelier—the true hip spot in Vermont—was most definitely one of the greatest experiences that I have had in my life. The job gave me both freedom and avid concentration, humor and drama. Evenings at the Savoy were my design and sketch time; restock time; popcorn-popping time; butter-melting time; Toblerone time (yum); preview peek time; laughing with co-workers time; renting R-rated movies underage time. My love for the Savoy is a lasting piece of me, and I will constantly remember it as the base of who I am today."

Hannah Woodard: "As a teenager I felt honored to be a part of the Savoy community behind the scenes. It offered a rare opportunity to immerse myself in other cultures and human experiences from around the world through film. Contributing to such an important staple of our community gave me a great sense of satisfaction and pride. I find myself sharing Savoy experiences as an adult and still feel that pride today (over sixteen years later)! The film festival in particular was one of my favorite parts of the program. I recall one year when warm weather came unexpectedly early. Between the melting snow and constant stream of new faces in the theater I remember feeling a renewed sense of optimism and inspiration for the future. It's a moment I still reflect on with fondness and gratitude for everything that came together to bring that event to Vermonters."

CHAPTER 22

"YOU MUST REMEMBER THIS..."

I t would take a lot of hours to figure out exactly how many films were shown at the Savoy during the twenty-nine years I was there. I can only estimate roughly that there were upward of two thousand. For many of these titles, there are memories and associations that have remained with me: I can't hear any mention of Akira Kurosawa's *Dersu Uzala* without recalling that it was the first time we received a print in such rough shape that we had to demand a new one. When I see a reference to Andrzej Wajda's *Man of Marble* or Tony Richardson's *Tom Jones*, I remember the only two instances when an electrical storm knocked out all of downtown Montpelier's power, canceling our shows. *Whose Life Is It Anyway?*, with Richard Dreyfuss, marked the first (but not the only) time, shortly after our 1981 opening, that only one person showed up for a show. I asked our lone customer, Mary Messier, if there was another time she might come, but her nursing schedule meant this Sunday late show was her only chance. The show must go on! And it did. When I think of that heartwarming (and sometimes scary) 1943 classic *Lassie Come Home*, I remember five-year-old Zephyr Billingsley in her mother's arms, carried wailing from the theater. About ten years later, Zephyr became one of our teenage popcorn scoopers, and about fifteen years after that she was bringing her own son to the Savoy matinees.

So when a title comes up in conversation and I find myself smiling—or sometimes grimacing—I'm often not calling up the film itself, but remembering a specific incident when it played at the theater. I think about the wide variety of films we showed, the people of all ages in our community that I got to know, and the role the Savoy played as a community gathering place and cultural mecca.

Here are a few more of those episodes.

Taste of Cherry

Lassie's ordeal was too much for some youngsters.

For a few years in the late 1990s and early 2000s, the Savoy presented a weekend afternoon series that featured excellent foreign language films. We had gauged that, unlike higher-profile foreign titles like *Pelle the Conqueror* (from Denmark) or *Life Is Beautiful* (from Italy), these particular films would not financially warrant a week's run. But they might draw sixty or seventy film buffs, which (with some sponsorship) was enough to schedule afternoon shows on Saturday and Sunday. Some excellent films were featured in that series: Tom Tykwer's German thriller *The Princess and the Warrior*, Søren Kragh-Jacobsen's unusual Danish drama *Mifune*, and Majid Majidi's touching Iranian film *The Color of Paradise*.

Another Iranian film one weekend was Abbas Kiarostami's *Taste of Cherry*. Although Kiarostami had been making films since the mid-1970s, it wasn't until *Taste of Cherry* that he had his first American art house success. The film starts with a middle-aged man, Mr. Badhi, driving his car through Tehran and its outskirts. He then picks up passenger after passenger to ask a great favor of them: to bury his body in the morning after he commits suicide. They all refuse. One young soldier flees at the weirdness of the request, a seminary student has religious objections, and a taxidermist tries to convince Mr. Badhi of the beauty of life.

I had been the projectionist the night before, showing our main feature, Woody Allen's *Celebrity*. A mistake I made in the booth that night didn't become clear until late Saturday afternoon, when I got a panicked call from Carlos Haase, who was projecting *Taste of Cherry*. I had mislabeled the reels, and he therefore had begun the Kiarostami film in the middle. Perhaps our savvy audience knew that Iranian films tended to unfold in an unusual narrative style. But no one, it seemed, realized anything was wrong until the end credits (in Persian) started rolling forty-five minutes earlier than they should have.

"What should I do?" asked Carlos. I suggested that he explain to the audience what had happened and offer to show the first half of the film to those who wanted to stay. Those who didn't could get a refund. An hour later, he called back: no one left, and the audience applauded at the "end." Now there's devotion.

Fear and Loathing in Las Vegas

For a while, several Savoy staff members lived on the third floor of the theater building. If there was a snowstorm in Calais on a Saturday morning, Michael Macomber was willing to open the video store (in his pajamas) and stay until we got there. Projectionist Hugo Martínez Cazón found it convenient to start heating his lunch in his apartment and then go two flights down to tend to the projection booth in the theater. When the film was underway, he'd go back to retrieve his lunch and bring it down to the booth.

On this particular Saturday, Hugo started projecting *The Wind in the Willows*, which we were showing for a children's matinee. Midway through the first reel, he left to heat his lunch, came back downstairs, and threaded up the second reel. After the changeover (from one projector to the next), he went upstairs again to get his lunch, and when he came back down he discovered he had mistakenly set up that night's feature on the second projector: *Fear and Loathing in Las Vegas*, with Johnny

Depp as Raoul Duke (a thinly disguised version of Hunter S. Thompson). This was decidedly not children's matinee fare due to prodigious drug use throughout the film.

They say that the job of the projectionist is long stretches of boredom interspersed with short episodes of panic. Hugo remembered his panic: "I am responsible for ALL of their little souls that moment, as Raoul Duke's open convertible drove down Route 66!!! Yikes!!! There was only one thing I could do that would immediately stop the kids from seeing anything they shouldn't." Instantly, he cut the power and the entire theater went dark, with only the exit lights remaining. "For a second," Hugo recalled, "the room was black as ink and totally silent." He then turned the power back on and brought up the house lights. Then, he said, "I burst through the swinging doors at the back of the theater, and ran into the room of now screaming children and bewildered adults, explaining there was a little technical problem and it would be fixed in a few minutes." Meanwhile, his lunch was cooling in the projection booth.

The Ruling Class / The Cook, The Thief, His Wife & Her Lover

One of the pleasures of managing the Savoy was talking, however briefly, with patrons as they left the theater. I almost always felt some investment in what we were showing and I was eager to hear their reactions. I can only remember two instances when I took to the safety of the projection booth rather than engage with the customers on their way out.

Once was when we showed the British comedy *The Ruling Class*, in which Peter O'Toole's mad aristocrat believes he is Jesus Christ. He is eventually cured of that particular delusion, but instead becomes convinced he is Jack the Ripper. I had been hearing about this 1972 film for years and hoped for a cult hit when we finally showed it ten years later. But the film was a flat and unfunny disappointment to me. When I finally read Roger Ebert's review in the *Chicago Sun-Times*, I agreed completely: "It indulges in scenes of fantasy and hallucination, often a sign of desperation in a comedy. It becomes very dark and violent and, even worse, it meanders. We get no real feeling that it knows where it's going, and every good comedy needs a certain headlong conviction."

As the film drew to a close, I dreaded what I thought was an inevitable question: "You thought THAT was funny?"

It happened again in 1989. One of the hit films of the year—critically, anyway—was Peter Greenaway's *The Cook, The Thief, His Wife & Her Lover*. It had a top-flight cast, including Michael Gambon ("the thief") and Helen Mirren ("his wife"), and was praised for its vivid production design. Writing in the *New York Times*, Caryn James called it "a work so intelligent and powerful that it evokes our best emotions and least civil impulses, so esthetically brilliant that it expands the boundaries of film itself." That review was good enough to warrant a run at the Savoy, though none of us had seen it beforehand.

If we had seen it on one of our movie-scouting trips to New York, Andrea and I might well have said, "Not for our audience." We might have agreed with a passionately negative review, written by Owen Gleiberman of *Entertainment Today*: "It's a hideously cruel revenge melodrama, an exploitation fantasy done with bodily fluids instead of guns. The final effect is deliberately repulsive enough to have won the film an X rating for its 'overall tone.'"

As a rule, our audience did not shy away from films that were artistically challenging, but a film so relentlessly unpleasant was a significant departure from the usual Savoy fare. Fortunately, there were no lasting ill effects on our attendance (such as "I'm never coming back here!"). Some of my friends who also ran small theaters seemed to delight in aggressively challenging their audience's comfort level ("You didn't like it? Tough luck!") But I had never developed the thick shell that they did—and didn't want to.

Breaking the Waves

Lars von Trier's breakthrough film got a rapturous reception at the 1996 New York Film Festival. Janet Maslin wrote, "Risky does not begin to describe *Breaking the Waves*, the raw, crazy tour de force that is the frenzied highlight of the festival this year." The film starred Stellan Skarsgård as Jan, an oil rig worker who marries Bess, a quiet, religious Scottish girl, played by Emily Watson. An accident leaves Jan paralyzed; Bess goes off the deep end and the film follows her.

Maslin noted the film's cinematography: "The film's visceral effectiveness is heightened further by the intimacy of Robby Muller's vigorous hand-held cinematography." On our opening night, we discovered that one person's "vigorous" is another person's "nauseating." All the customers in the Savoy's first seven rows quickly changed seats once the film began, literally unable to maintain their equilibrium. On later, crowded nights, those trapped up front asked for a refund or rain check. It was the only film we ever showed that literally made people sick.

Some viewers also chose to exit as the film entered its second hour and von Trier ratcheted up the punishing drama of Bess's degradation. Andrea and I were in the video store one night when a distraught customer came downstairs. He said, "I just want to know, does anything bad happen to her when she gets on that boat?" He was referring to Bess's making herself sexually available to her husband's crewmates. Andrea asked in return, "Do you mean the first or the second time?" He was horrified: "Oh no, you mean there's a second time?" That was enough for him to skip the rest of the movie.

My Own Private Idaho

In 1991, we had a rare hit film, Gus Van Sant's *My Own Private Idaho*. Even rarer, it brought in a younger audience. Van Sant had been making excellent low-budget features in his home city of Portland, Oregon. Despite the rough subject matter of this film—young gay hustlers on the streets of Portland—Van Sant finally broke through to a wider audience.

He was aided, no doubt, by the presence of two popular young actors, River Phoenix and Keanu Reeves, who bravely surrendered themselves to Van Sant's vision. Roger Ebert, in one of the film's many excellent reviews, defined that vision as "a human comedy, a story that may be sad and lonely in parts but is illuminated by the insight that all experience is potentially ridiculous; that if we could see ourselves with enough detachment, some of the things we take with deadly seriousness might seem more than faintly absurd."

What makes Phoenix's character Mike so unusual is that he suffers from narcolepsy. As Ebert points out, "To those who do not

she refused to give up her bus seat, is in Phoenix to honor slain civil rights leader, Dr. Martin Luther King Jr.

STARTS TONIGHT • 6:30 • 8:40

"The best American movie of the Nineties!"
- Donald Lyons, FILM COMMENT

★★★★! **Exceptional** . . . so delightfully different and daring that it renews your faith." Marshall Fine, GANNETT NEWS SERVICE

RIVER PHOENIX   KEANU REEVES

MY OWN PRIVATE IDAHO

A FILM BY GUS VAN SANT

THE SAVOY THEATER
26 Main Street • Montpelier • Vermont • 229-0509

Life imitated art for *My Own Private Idaho.*

understand the disorder, it appears that he must be on drugs, or mentally deficient, or from another planet. His condition has given him a certain dreamy detachment; there is no use getting too deeply involved in events you may end up sleeping through."

On the busy Saturday night of opening weekend, as the credits were rolling, it was time for me to turn on the overhead lights halfway and open the doors for the exiting audience. I noticed there was an unusual traffic jam at the rear exit. People seemed to be avoiding something in the aisle: a closer look revealed that it was a teenager, fast asleep on the floor. I was relieved when my gentle prodding woke him out of his stupor. I didn't inquire too closely about whether life was imitating art.

On another night of that week's run, the "mixed precipitation" so dreaded by Vermonters created uniquely hazardous conditions. First there was snow, then rain, then a freeze, covering everything in a glaze of ice. Our car was parked almost directly in front of the theater, but we could not imagine how we could safely walk there from the theater door. It was one of the rare nights we stayed with friends in Montpelier; we weren't even tempted to try the twenty-minute drive home. How our customers all got home I'll never know.

The Gods Must Be Crazy

On most weeks, receiving a film for a Friday opening was a matter of routine. George and Doris Tremblay owned a company called Film Express of New England, one of the many small ancillary businesses dependent on the film industry. On four days of the week, George worked in construction, but on Thursdays he picked up films—including ours— at a Boston depot used by many film distributors as a pickup point for delivery to theaters from Maine to Rhode Island. George had a route that took him from Boston to Burlington, Vermont, and back, dropping off films and concession goods along the way, then picking up the "ends Thursday" films on his way home.[39]

On Wednesday mornings, we'd call Doris to alert her which film we were expecting from which distributor at the Boston depot the next day. Sometimes, though, instead of seeing our film cans in the Savoy lobby on a Friday morning, there would be a note from George. This is how we would discover at nine a.m. that our film was coming in by bus or Fed Ex or a private courier. This dreaded development always involved much hand-wringing and impromptu schedule rearrangement. On one particular Friday, we learned that we'd have to pick up that night's film, *The Gods Must Be Crazy*, at 4:30 at the Montpelier Greyhound station.

We were anticipating a busy run for this South African comedy, which became a surprise international hit in 1980 and 1981. The storyline of writer-director Jamie Uys's film involved a Kalahari bushman who discovers a Coca-Cola bottle in the desert. As they say, complications ensue.[40]

We could not preview the film that afternoon. With the late arrival, Chris Wood was barely able to thread up the film just as the crowd started arriving. I didn't watch the film that night, content to sit in the lobby and

[39]George had been delivering our films for years when we discovered that on some later-than-usual Thursdays, he spent the night in the theater. One Friday morning, I came in and immediately sensed that I wasn't alone. There was George in his portable cot, sleeping in the aisle.

[40]It was only after we showed the film that we discovered it had become a source of controversy. It was condemned (and picketed in some cases) for the perceived perpetuation of racial stereotypes and ignorance of discrimination and apartheid in South Africa.

listen to the constant laughter drifting out. But when the film changed over to the second projector, there was a roar unlike any in the first half.

What could be so funny?

It was reel four, upside down. It took some doing to make right—cutting and rewinding and splicing and recutting and resplicing. It was a good lesson in why you should always preview a film before presenting it to an audience—and what can go wrong when you don't.

Fahrenheit 911

In December 2003, Howard Dean, former Vermont governor and then-current presidential candidate, took a lot of criticism for what proved to be a prescient observation: that the capture of Iraqi leader Saddam Hussein did not make our country safer. By spring of 2004, Dean had been proved correct; the cracks were beginning to show in the false "weapons of mass destruction" cover story for the beginning of the war. Our entire (three-strong) congressional delegation was opposed to the Iraq War, but many Vermonters felt they and other war opponents were shouting into a void.

AROUND THE BLOCKBUSTER

The Savoy Theater's sold-out first showing of Michael Moore's "Farenheit 911" began at 6:30 p.m. Friday. About 100 disappointed movie-goers eagerly waited for the 9 p.m. showing. A line extending along an entire block on Main Street in Montpelier formed early as people came out to see the Cannes Film Festival winner. No advance tickets are for sale.

Every theater owner's dream — a line down the block.

This was the backdrop for the summer 2004 release of Michael Moore's documentary *Fahrenheit 911*. The Savoy had done well with Moore's previous films, *Roger and Me* and *Bowling for Columbine*, so we were looking forward to big crowds.[41]

The film was merciless in its exposure of George W. Bush's dishonesty and incompetence. In its examination of the aftermath of the attacks of 9/11, the film was an insightful exposé of the ties between the Bush family and the Saudi rulers who financed Osama Bin Laden. For once, we had underestimated how popular a film would be. It seemed that for many moviegoers, buying a ticket to see this film was tantamount to protesting in front of the White House.

Lines down the block—every theater-owner's dream—greeted us on our first Saturday afternoon for the first of four sold-out shows that day. So did a pelting rainstorm. We dragged every umbrella we could find out of our lost-and-found stash and then went across the street to Capitol Stationers to buy its entire stock of golf umbrellas. We handed one to every fifth person, recycling them to the back of the line as the crowd came forward.

Fahrenheit 911 played for five weeks. It didn't make any difference as far as ending the war, which dragged on many more years, but it was a vivid lesson in the power of an engaged filmmaker to reach a large audience. I'll always remember those umbrellas when I think of Moore's film.

Hardly Gold

For a few years in the late 1990s, Andrea organized a well-attended children's series at the Savoy on Saturday mornings. One of those screenings featured a special guest or, more accurately, a guest and her owner.

Chundo was one of the litter of Fay Ray, the Weimaraner made famous by the photographer and filmmaker William Wegman. Wegman delighted in dressing his pliant dogs in costumes of all sorts and posing them in unusual positions. Chundo and Fay, along with Chundo's siblings Battina and Crooky, graced a poster for the 1992 New York Film Festival

---

[41]My favorite customer inquiry came from a caller wondering if we were going to show Moore's film *Bowling for Concubine*.

that showed them sitting in theater seats. That poster hung for many years in the Savoy lobby, a gift from William Wegman's sister Pam, who lived in Montpelier at the time.

When we discovered that William Wegman had made a short film starring this canine family, it was natural to include it in our children's series. The film, *Hardly Gold,* was shot on Rangeley Lake in Maine and starred the four Weimaraners as the "Hardly Boys," dressed in their finest L.L. Bean outfits. Taking off on the classic F.W. Dixon *The Hardy Boys* books, the film had the four dogs solve various mysteries in and around their cabin (actually the Wegman family vacation home), with William Wegman himself delivering a deadpan narration.

Pam Wegman was delighted with the idea of showing the film with Chundo in attendance. We advertised that one of the stars of the film would be on hand to greet the audience afterward. The film went well. Pam and Chundo waited patiently in the lobby for the film to end. Once

Hardly Gold: a celebrated dog put in a Savoy appearance.

it was over, though, we realized that we had lost sight of an important fact, namely that Chundo was a dog. The open theater doors were all the invitation that Chundo needed to patrol the aisles, searching out spilled popcorn. Like our own black lab, Bessie (who often "cleaned" the theater in between shows), Chundo was more interested in the popcorn on the floor than the children who rushed after her to give her a quick pat.

Next Stop, Greenwich Village

When Paul Mazursky died in 2014, the *New York Times* capsule epitaph read, "Captured the Me Era's Strengths and Foibles." The writer was no doubt thinking of films like *Bob & Carol & Ted & Alice, Alex in Wonderland,* and *Blume in Love.* But to me, I think of Mazursky primarily as someone who mined the Jewish experience in twentieth century America.

Mazursky was first an actor and then a television writer before becoming a film director. He was inspired by films like François Truffaut's *The 400 Blows* and Federico Fellini's *8 1/2,* which were frankly autobiographical. *Next Stop, Greenwich Village* is the story of one year, 1953, in which the young proto-Mazursky named Lenny Lapinsky leaves a stifling Brooklyn household to move to Greenwich Village. By the end of the film, he is ready to move to Hollywood (in real life, he got a part in *The Blackboard Jungle*).

Mazursky told Roger Ebert that "it's a very personal film,

Milton Glaser's brilliant poster for *Next Stop Greenwich Village.*

even though it shouldn't be seen as literal autobiography." He also noted that his film is "more *inspired* by his years in the Village than *based* on them." His portrait of the Village in the early 1950s is bursting with energy, humor, and occasional pathos. Among the many denizens of Lenny's local bar is an overbearing, womanizing sculptor named Barney, portrayed by the playwright John Ford Noonan.

A month before the Savoy scheduled *Next Stop, Greenwich Village*, I read that Noonan was going to be nearby for most of the summer. I forget how I contacted him, but he was happy to speak at one showing of the film. A large man with a personality to match, Noonan had the audience laughing from the start of his introduction.

When the film started, he came out to the lobby and asked for a restaurant recommendation. "What time do I have to be back?" he asked me. I told him, adding that he could come back any time before that. He could sit in the audience and see how the audience was appreciating the film. He shocked me with his answer: "I've never seen the film." I must have appeared stupefied, since he quickly explained, "I had such a good time shooting it, I want to keep those memories fresh."

Life Cycles: Casablanca /
The Life and Times of Hank Greenberg

We almost had a birth in the theater. To mark the Savoy's fifth, tenth, and then, in 1996, fifteenth anniversary, we hosted a free showing of *Casablanca*. It was a high-spirited day at the theater, with people returning to see the film for their second, fifth, or tenth time. The *Times Argus* quoted a Burlington regular, Mark Green, as saying he passed up a trip to the slopes on this sunny January day to see the film for his seventeenth time: "It's *the* movie, and it's *the* theater."

The film proceeded for a packed house, but before Rick Blaine could put Ilsa Lund and Victor Laszlo on the plane, a couple I knew got up and bolted out through the doors. Terry Solomon and Emily Sloan barely had a chance to say "It's happening!" as they rushed out of the theater to get to the hospital in time. And I didn't have the chance to ask if they would consider "Rick" and "Ilsa" as possible names for their baby. (She was named "Julia," as it turned out.)

An upsetting occasion at the other end of the life cycle occurred in July 2000. With the elderly patrons who regularly made up a good part of our audience, we were always a little nervous at the prospect of one of them dying in the theater. But when it finally happened, it was not a senior but a forty-nine-year-old: a well-loved physician named Gary Zaret. Gary had a fatal aneurysm, sitting in the back of the theater during a showing of Aviva Kempner's *The Life and Times of Hank Greenberg.*

It had started out as a special night at the Savoy, with two speakers lined up for that show. Dave "Boo" Ferriss had been a pitcher for the Boston Red Sox and, in his rookie year, was one of the last pitchers to face Greenberg, the Detroit Tigers' legendary slugger, when Greenberg was in his final season. The Vermont Historical Society was hosting a summer-long baseball exhibit and "Boo" was in Montpelier to take part. Our old friend Henry Sapoznik had composed the score for the documentary, and he was on hand, too, eager to share stories of that experience.

About halfway through the show, someone seated toward the rear of the theater rushed out and said that it looked like the person seated in front of him had fainted. I called for an ambulance, which arrived within minutes. We stopped the film and turned up the lights. I announced— without any explanation—that there would be a short break. I discovered later that those sitting closer to the front had no idea that anything unusual had happened.

It took less than five minutes for the crew to carry Gary out of the theater, and we learned the next day that he had died shortly after arriving at the hospital. Andrea and Henry had gone out for dinner during that show. When they returned, they took one look at my ashen face and knew something terrible had happened.

CHAPTER 23

SLOW FADE

A phone call in 2006 stays in my mind as an omen of the end of my years at the Savoy. A long box-office drought ended with our booking *The Queen*, starring Helen Mirren as Queen Elizabeth II. We fully expected a hit and weren't disappointed, given our track record with *Enchanted April*, *Ladies in Lavender*, *Tea with Mussolini*, and *Mrs. Brown*. All of these films were genteel British comedy/dramas appealing to a certain portion of the Savoy audience (read: over fifty and mainly women). I was talking to fellow theater-owner Steve Lieber, of Upstate Films in Rhinebeck, New York. Steve, who was also showing *The Queen*, commented, "I'm not sure who's going to die first, us or our audience."

That was the challenge, in a nutshell. The Savoy was counting on Judi Dench, Maggie Smith, Anthony Hopkins, and Helen Mirren just as more mainstream theaters counted on Brad Pitt, Jennifer Lopez, or George Clooney. Our audience was getting older, and at the same time, there seemed to be nothing we could do to draw a younger crowd. Once in a while, some teenagers would show up to see *Little Miss Sunshine* or *Slumdog Millionaire*. Films like *River's Edge* or *Heathers* were ostensibly about teenagers, but were perceived as being art house films. The Savoy never was able to shake an elitist image that kept teens away. Once,

I asked our teenage concession staff member Sophie Miles if there was anything we could do to attract her age group. She shook her head and told me, "I hate to break it to you, but the truth is that all my peers have been conditioned to want to see crap."

We knew there were good films to show. However, many high-quality films did not draw sufficient crowds. Philip Seymour Hoffman won the Best Actor Oscar for *Capote,* and the film had garnered national attention. And yet our attendance was disappointing. This surprised us, for Montpelier is a literate and literary town. Did people feel that they weren't familiar enough with Capote's work to appreciate the film? Or that some found him an unappealing subject? At times like these I ruefully remembered the words of the colorful Russian-born impresario Sol Hurok: "If people don't want to go to something, nothing on earth is going to stop them."[42]

More excellent films, more disappointing turnouts: *The Savages* (with Laura Linney) and *Away from Her* (with Julie Christie) received excellent press, but the subjects they explored—aging and dementia—were not appealing. *A History of Violence* was hailed as one of David Cronenberg's best, but the title itself was enough to keep people away. *Half Nelson,* with Ryan Gosling, was one of the best indies to come along in a while, but its urban setting and theme of drug addiction was a turnoff that no amount of national press or personal word-of-mouth could overcome.

Perhaps even a national campaign could not convince the Central Vermont audience to take a chance on a film, like *Away from Her* or *Half Nelson,* perceived as "difficult" or "depressing." How many did times did I hear the refrain, "I see enough of that in the news"? Though the Green Mountain Film Festival often drew robust crowds for timely, serious films, the story at the Savoy was different. A festival was a special event, whereas a night at the movies often called for escapist fare.

In addition, our choices of what to play were limited at the outset. We were dependent on the slate of releases by independent distributors

---

[42]The corollary was stated by Oscar Hammerstein, not the famous lyricist but his father, who had been a Broadway producer: "The number of people who decide not to attend any given event turns out to be infinite."

The Queen: "Who's going to die first?"

such as Sony Classics, Miramax, and October Films. They, too, had their slow periods when there was not much that was appealing. In such cases, we had to make our best guesses (aided by advice from our booker, Jeffrey Jacobs) about what films just might do well—or well enough. We were rarely in a position to book a film released by a major studio (like Paramount or Columbia) that had a national publicity campaign with television advertising.

And then there were the Oscars, which became the bane of our existence for a few months each year from late November to March. Both studio and independent distributors often saved their "prestige pictures" for the fall and early winter, hoping to take advantage of best-of-the-year-list momentum. Jeffrey would convey the messages from Sony Classics or Fox Searchlight: "No, you can't have *Atonement* until the nominations are announced" or "Now that our film has five nominations, we won't take less than a four-week run." Then there was the time, in 2006, when we booked the comedy *Sideways*, set in California's wine country. It filled our Thanksgiving-to-Christmas slot well, but the film didn't get that Oscar buzz until after the new year, well after we had sent it back. Just our luck!

Our worst Oscar experience came in February 2008. We had an enormous Christmas hit with the poignant comedy *Juno*, which was just tapering off in its fifth week at the Savoy when the nominations were announced. We were scheduled to open *Atonement*, the World War II–era romance based on Ian McEwan's award-winning novel, that Friday. *Juno* received four nominations, including Best Picture and Best Actress (Ellen Page), and *Atonement* got seven. Fox Searchlight, the distributor of *Juno*, wanted us to play its film another week, while Focus Features, the distributor of *Atonement*, wanted us to open that film right away. If we had had a second screen, it would have provided an easy solution: put *Juno* in the smaller theater for another week. Ultimately, we took Jeffrey's advice ("You don't want to piss off Searchlight"). We reluctantly took the sixth week of *Juno* and watched *Atonement* open down the street a few days later. Once again, I cursed the Oscars and their dominance of the marketplace.

Keeping *Juno*, losing *Atonement*.

•

We also had to deal with an ever-evolving technology and media landscape. An explosion of cable channels and affordable high-defini-tion televisions (HDTV) meant that people could enjoy seemingly infinite ways to find entertainment at home. Our membership remained steady but declining attendance created an ever-widening deficit.

We were excited to learn of a new restaurant, Claire's, in nearby Hardwick, that used a community-based financial model. We talked with Paul Bruhn and Ann Cousins at the Preservation Trust of Vermont, who had helped organize Claire's as a restaurant owned by its community investors/patrons—a more ambitious version of what we had done with our membership structure. Paul and Ann generated some excellent ideas, but Andrea and I realized it was too late in the game (and we were twenty years too old) to implement them. We were putting too much energy into how to meet our payroll and pay our distributors. Long-range planning could not be a priority.

We had always assumed we'd keep operating the Savoy until we were seventy. But the rocky finances of the theater and video store were causing us to reconsider. We hadn't formulated any particular plans, but we asked our longtime friends and theater supporters Jane and Ed Pincus to meet with us. The Pincuses had both been involved with the arts and with nonprofit organizations for many years; we thought they might have some ideas about how best to navigate our uncertain future.

Ed was very direct. "At least find out if there's a buyer out there," he said. "Contact a business broker." Gulp! Really? "You'll know where you stand. If no one is interested, then we can talk about Plan B." It was not what we expected to hear. Andrea and I had a soul-searching conversation on our way back from Pincus Road in Roxbury. We acknowledged that the financial struggles of the theater were taking an emotional toll on both of us.

By the next morning we had set up an appointment with John and Sharon Beal at Vermont Business Brokers. When they visited the theater, John and Sharon were somewhat nonplussed at the prospect of putting a price tag on the Savoy. It was a retail business but didn't sell any tangible goods. Like other businesses, it had fixed inventory—like projectors and seats (and that popcorn machine!)—and year-end financial statements. But how to put a number on what a place means to a community? The Beals had never helped sell a theater before, but they came to enjoy the challenge that the Savoy brought.

When the news that the Savoy was on the market went public in late July 2009, the *Times Argus* quoted John Beal as saying, "It's a pleasure to walk into something where somebody has had so much pride and respect in it. It's a unique opportunity that fills a narrow niche." The article concluded by quoting Andrea: "I find it rather telling that neither Rick nor I has had a single second thought. It's clearly the right thing to do." By late August, we had a buyer, Terry Youk, a documentary filmmaker who lived in Montpelier.[43]

No one who has sold a house, let alone a business, will be surprised to know that the details of the sale took another five months to settle. Our last week as owners coincided with one of the traditionally slowest times of the year: the week before Christmas. Andrea and I took the opportunity to schedule a week of old foreign language favorites as a way of saying farewell: Akira Kurosawa's *Yojimbo*, Federico Fellini's *The White Sheik*, Ingmar Bergman's *Wild Strawberries*, and (of course) Marcel Carné and Jacques Prévert's *Children of Paradise*.

One of the first decisions that Terry faced as the new owner of the Savoy during his first year involved even more recent

Rick Winston is selling the Savoy Theater in Montpelier. He owns the theater with his wife, Andrea Sirota. Winston came to Vermont in 1970 to visit friends at Goddard College and stayed.

Savoy Theater for sale

Winston opened movie house in 1980

By Sally Pollak
Free Press Staff Writer

The Savoy Theater, a cinema on Main Street in Montpelier, is for sale, co-owner Rick Winston said.

Winston, who turned 62 Wednesday, owns the theater with his wife, Andrea Serota, who turns 62 today.

"We don't want to keep running it until we have absolutely no energy," Winston said. "We'd like to ensure, while we're still active, to put the energy into paving the way so that the institution will keep going and perhaps thrive."

Winston has been presenting films in Montpelier since 1972, when his weekly film society, Lightning Ridge (named for the road where he lives in Calais), showed movies in the basement of the Pavilion building.

"I'd lug in 16mm projectors and throw the film onto the white wall," he said.

In 1980, with two partners, he opened the

Savoy. Their plan was to show a mix of classic and contemporary films, Winston said.

"It became obvious within five or six months that it really was the newer films people wanted to see," Winston said. "After we showed two films, 'Return of the Secaucus Seven' and 'My Brilliant Career,' we were sort of off and running."

Now showing at the Savoy: "Food, Inc."

The sale of the Savoy includes the DVD rental shop beneath the theater, Downstairs Video.

If a sale of the business goes through, part of the agreement would be that the Green Mountain Film Festival will take place in March 2010, Winston said. In addition, all Savoy memberships will be honored, he said.

People interested in purchasing the Savoy should contact Vermont Business Brokers in Charlotte, Winston said. He declined to name a purchase price.

Theater for sale — Front page news!

technological advances: the transition from 35-millimeter film to digital projection. By the end of 2011, there would be no more "Goldberg" cans or splicing tables. When Terry told me what it would cost to refit the projection booth, I must admit I understood the relief of those who sold all their stocks in September 1929.[44]

---

[43]In 2016, Terry sold the theater to James O'Hanlon.

[44]Terry also wrought a change Andrea and I had never considered possible: the conversion of the downstairs space into a cozy thirty-five-seat screening room. Terry had moved Downstairs Video down the street, but soon "the html was on the wall," as a friend said. Facing the growing popularity of streaming services, Downstairs Video closed for good in 2011.

Andrea and I had no idea how we would feel once the theater and video store were no longer ours. It didn't take long—in fact, the first Monday without a payroll to meet—to realize the truth of the maxim, "You never know how heavy the burden is until it's lifted off your shoulders." I was continuing my involvement in the festival and teaching a weekly film class for the Montpelier Senior Activity Center, but Andrea gave herself the luxury to do nothing except read and garden for six months.

People often ask us, "Do you miss the theater?" The answer is a mixed one. We certainly haven't missed the financial worries or the late nights. But we have missed the camaraderie of our theater family and the weekly contact with our many film-loving friends in the community.

Andrea and I — saying farewell, 2009.

2007 Green Mountain Film Festival cover art by Hal Mayforth.

PART
6

THE SHOW *DOES*
GO ON!

CHAPTER 24

"WHAT'S A CUT?"
AND OTHER QUESTIONS

I had an opportunity to teach at the Community College of Vermont in Montpelier in 2013. This came at a fortunate juncture for me, as it was my first year without an income from the Green Mountain Film Festival.

Fortunately, CCV (as it is known) recognized my real-world experience and, unlike some other Vermont educational institutions, did not require its instructors to have an advanced degree. I wouldn't dare compare myself to the poet Allen Ginsberg, but he faced a similar problem at my almost alma mater Columbia University. Despite his worldwide fame, he was told by the Columbia administration: no PhD, no class. (Brooklyn College quickly hired him.)

Elizabeth King, CCV's coordinator of academic services, offered me a summer class teaching Introduction to Film Studies 101. That sounded good—but it was not your ordinary summer class. CCV was experimenting with cramming the usual thirteen weeks of summer classes into seven weeks (a schedule known as Summer Intensive), with one six-hour class per week.

I was already apprehensive about teaching younger students, unlike my usual over-sixty students. But six hours? That is a lot of time for a class, even with showing a two-hour film. I held my panic at bay, while I read the CCV handbook and consulted some experienced CCV hands

I knew: my sister-in-law Suzanne Rexford-Winston, who taught art; my friend Kathleen Moore, who taught English; and my film festival comrade Dianne Maccario, then a CCV administrator. Through them I discovered that part of the solution to my six-hour problem was right there in the CCV ethos: get the students involved—get their help in using those six hours well.

At the end of the first class, I assigned each of the students to research one silent film director: D.W. Griffith, Charlie Chaplin, Buster Keaton, Cecil B. DeMille, Sergei Eisenstein, et al. They also watched both *Singin' in the Rain* and *Sunset Boulevard* at home, both of which—in very different ways—deal with the transition from silent films to sound.

On returning to class, each student gave a report on the particular director from the silent era and I would show a short clip. Then I had them break into three small groups to discuss questions about *Singin' in the Rain* and *Sunset Boulevard*:

- What are the expectations we bring to these two films?
- Do we expect to enjoy them in different ways?
- Which of these two films are you more likely to want to see again, tell friends about, or talk about? Why?
- What were some of the key scenes in each film?
- Was their effectiveness due to the script, the choices the director made, the acting, or a combination?
- What did you learn about the world of silent films?

The breakout groups lasted for thirty minutes, and then each group reported back to the entire class. The six hours suddenly seemed a lot less onerous.

I took the "Introduction" part of the class title as literally as I could. If one is used to being a passive viewer, never thinking about what goes into making a film, where does an instructor start? In my case, with the vocabulary: what is a pan? a cut? a tracking shot? What's the job of the editor or cinematographer?

In other words, what is the grammar of film?

We watched clips that used examples, including the camera pan around the cowboys in *Red River*, the fifty-plus cuts in the telephone

Singin' in the Rain: "What a glorious feeling..."

booth scene of *The Birds* (we counted them aloud), and the tracking shot following Bonnie and Clyde's first conversation. In this way I could mix in some film history, introducing the students to directors such as Howard Hawks, Alfred Hitchcock, and Arthur Penn.

One week I invited film history instructor Barry Snyder of Burlington College to discuss foreign films with me, and another week, the Norwich, Vermont, filmmaker Nora Jacobson conveyed to the class the unique struggles of making independent features.

By the end of the seven weeks, I no longer felt burdened by the six-hour slot. The students had been on an accelerated journey from the silent film era through the Golden Age of Hollywood to the rise of independent film, with many side trips. During our final session, the students talked a little about what they had learned. One comment I particularly remember—and cherish—was "Before this class, I never used to pay any attention to the credits. Now I have a greater appreciation of what all those jobs are."

I didn't want to let the summer go by without showing my CCV students at least one foreign film. My guess (correct, as it happened) was that hardly anyone in the class had ever seen an entire subtitled film. Why not throw them into the deep end of the pool with what might be the ultimate foreign film, Ingmar Bergman's 1957 classic *The Seventh Seal*?

How could anything be further away—in theme, setting, and style—from Hollywood movies?

The action of the film takes place hundreds of years before the first colonists arrived at Plymouth Rock; the characters earnestly philosophize about the meaning of God's will. On a minuscule budget, Bergman convincingly recreated the Middle Ages with the story of Antonius Block (Max von Sydow), a crusader who returns to Sweden only to be confronted with the figure of Death.

I thought about the first time I had seen *The Seventh Seal*, as a college freshman. I was stunned by the imagery but at a loss to understand much of the film. Thinking back on that experience, I wondered: what should I have known before walking into that auditorium cold?

I used that memory as the guideline for preparing my class. I handed out a short reading from Barbara Tuchman's *A Distant Mirror*, in which she described the religious fervor of the Crusades and how the Black Death spread across Europe. Tuchman explained how the Bible's Book of Revelations (from which Bergman's film takes its title) was "the favorite guide to human affairs" at the time.

I prepared the students for a disturbing scene with a procession of flagellants, who take the Black Death as a sign they are not pious enough. I prepped them on the place of the itinerant theater troupe in society; the figure of Death, which Bergman recreated from the medieval frescoes he had seen as a child; and the feudal structure which is conveyed in

The Seventh Seal:
traveling players
Jof and Mia.

the relationship between Max von Sydow's knight and Gunnar Björnstrand's squire. I suggested that Bergman's film could also be viewed through the prism of several modern genres, familiar to all the students: the road movie, the returning-vet film, and the disaster epic.

With that, we were ready to watch the film. I had forgotten about Bergman's earthy humor and was delighted to hear the students' laughter at several points during this otherwise somber tale. One thing I could observe from the back of the classroom was that no students were fidgeting or surreptitiously checking their phones.

My assignment for them was to write three pages, with two choices: "How does Bergman cinematically present the world that surrounds his hero? Which scenes were especially effective for you and why?" or "How does Bergman explore one of the following themes: the knight's loss of faith, fate versus free will, or good versus evil?"

When the assignments were handed in a week later, I was gratified by my students' willingness to engage with Bergman's vision. One student's response to the film has stayed with me. She identified herself as a devout Catholic and noted that although the Bergman film did not deal with Catholicism, it treated religious faith as something to take seriously—unlike what she called the dismissive treatment of religious people in most mainstream films. The characters in *The Seventh Seal* grappled with profound questions, giving her a movie-going experience that was fresh and meaningful.

I have noticed that some contemporary critics take a disdainful view of Bergman as a relic of a certain period when art house cinema carried a "more-intellectual-than-thou" cachet. David Thomson, in his Bergman entry in *The Biographical Dictionary of Film*, called *The Seventh Seal* "pretentious and calculating." He added, "Its medieval-ism and the wholesale allegory now seem frivolous and theatrical diversions from true seriousness." On the contrary, my experience introducing the film to young students only increased my appreciation of Bergman. As Andrew Sarris wrote in a 2007 column in the *New York Observer,* "We are reminded of what even the more skeptical among us have always loved and admired about Bergman's movies: humanity, humility, insight, intelligence and a heroic seriousness of purpose."

CHAPTER 25

BILL MORANCY,
A KINDRED SPIRIT

One summer in the mid-1990s, Andrea and I both became aware of a singular new video customer. Not a surprise: we tended to notice when someone would come in every few days, take out five foreign language films, and exclaim what superb taste we had!

That was Bill Morancy, who we quickly learned was in Vermont for a summer break from Martha's Vineyard. One of Bill's jobs there was as a housepainter. "Those rich people don't want to see a lowly housepainter during the summer," Bill explained. "The place is such a zoo in the summer I can't wait to get out."

He and his then-wife Betsy rented a house on Nelson Pond in South Woodbury for several summers in a row. During that time I got to discover more about Bill. He was a native of Pawtucket, Rhode Island, and of French-Canadian and Irish heritage. After an unsatisfying stint in the white-collar world (law and insurance), he moved to Martha's Vineyard, where he worked at a variety of jobs; besides the house painting, he had been a video store and bookstore clerk, baker, surveyor, and movie projectionist. He spearheaded a successful effort to establish a community radio station (WVVY) that is still thriving.

We had a rare winter visit from Bill once when he had a chance to buy an existing but shabby movie theater on "the island." But after some brain-picking sessions and phone calls back and forth, the opportunity fell through. After that, Bill disappeared for several summers.

Then one day in 2005, there he was, on the street in Montpelier. His marriage had broken up, and there was nothing keeping him on Martha's Vineyard. He thought of Montpelier and the welcoming atmosphere he had experienced. Within a week, he was learning the ropes in our projection booth. In the next few years he also worked as a clerk at Bear Pond Books, was a contestant at storytelling events, and one summer he even "ran away with the circus," manning the concession counter for the popular teen performing group Circus Smirkus.

Bill and I enjoyed many hours together in the Savoy lobby, in between screenings, when he projected and I scooped popcorn. We got to know each other's film tastes over those many evenings, discussing our favorite Kurosawa epics or films that critics seemed to love but we didn't (John Ford's *The Searchers* comes to mind).

When Andrea and I sold the Savoy in late 2009, I was approached by John Bloch, one of the prime movers behind Montpelier's public access television network, ORCA Media (Onion River Community Access). John wanted to know if I'd be interested in hosting a TV show about movies. The idea didn't appeal to me but I suggested he contact Bill. Bill didn't like the idea of a solo show either, but he came back to me with his own proposal: what if we did it together? We could create a public version of our lobby chats—Montpelier's own Gene Siskel and Roger Ebert, but not as combative or obnoxious.

We envisioned a series of half-hour episodes, each planned around a theme, with each of us selecting two clips to present. Our friend Eve Mendelsohn set up a video camera in Bill's living room for our first test run of *Talking About Movies*. In this "pilot" we talked about our early moviegoing experiences and, in particular, two films that have stayed with us through the years. If you've read this far, you won't be surprised to find out mine were *Rear Window* and *Citizen Kane*; Bill's were *The African Queen* (the first film his parents took him to see) and the sci-fi cult film *Forbidden Planet* (Bill had a much deeper appreciation of sci-fi and monster movies than I did). Our rough cut looked okay enough, so we went into the ORCA studios to do the real thing. It turned out to be

A characteristic Bill Morancy expression.

the first of more than two hundred *Talking About Movies* episodes that Bill and I did over a five-year period.

Once a month, we'd get together to plan our next four segments. Our topics ranged widely: appreciation of actors (Marcello Mastroianni), national cinemas (Iranian films), directors (Mira Nair), and off-beat subjects (motorcycle movies). During our first few months, we carefully planned who would say what about which film, but soon we settled into an unscripted, Savoy lobby-style give-and-take.

"We'll never run out of show ideas," Bill would often exult as we'd finish taping an ORCA segment. It was a characteristic expression of his joy at the prospect of sharing his enthusiasms with the world at large. We didn't run out of ideas, but Bill sadly ran out of time. One week we were playing tennis, and the next he was diagnosed with pancreatic cancer.

He rallied for one more program that November—on the actress Setsuko Hara and her work with the Japanese master director Yasujirō Ozu—but shortly afterward, he became too weak to do any more. Bill could not fathom a life without lively conversation among friends. Thanks to Vermont's Act 39 (technically the Patient Choice and Control at End of Life Act), Bill chose the day and time of his peaceful exit.

•

Bill stayed opinionated till the end. At a saying-goodbye party just a few days before his death, he insisted to Andrea that she was completely wrong in her negative opinion of Luchino Visconti's *The Leopard*: "How could you not appreciate such an obvious masterpiece?" He died in December 2015, just two months after recording our last ORCA segment.

The downstairs area at the Savoy is now called "The Morancy Screening Room." As one of his friends commented after Bill's death, "those of us who were near enough, geographically, to support Bill in his final months were struck by the variety and range of all who enjoyed and were affected by his personality and passions for film, adventure, good conversation, culture, and play."

CHAPTER 26

FURTHER FILM PLEASURES

Even as a youngster, I sensed that both my parents were generous and inspirational teachers. They believed that knowledge is inherently satisfying, but that the real joy lay in sharing it. And as art teachers specifically, they believed strongly in the power of the arts to transform students.

It was not unusual for some of these students to join us in Yonkers for a meal and a leisurely tour of my parents' art books. They would often stay in touch through college and onward, as they made their own careers in artistic endeavors. For example, Jean Krulis became a noted book designer, Steven Stipelman a fashion illustrator, and Georgeen Comerford a photojournalism professor.

I didn't realize how deeply I had absorbed my parents' ethos until I made my own gradual transition from film exhibitor to film historian and teacher. By the time we sold the theater in 2009, I was already involved in a number of film education endeavors.

•

One engagement that turned out to have lasting consequences was at Montpelier's Kellogg-Hubbard Library in 2004. Ellen Miles, a Savoy projectionist and at that time the library's events coordinator, asked me to present a film program of my choosing. The idea for the topic came after Andrea and I had watched a Bette Davis film from 1935 called *Dangerous* (Davis won the first of her two Oscars for it). As it ended, Andrea's verdict was "NOT a classic." We proceeded to have one of our periodic conversations about what makes some films classics while others, perhaps with the same stars or directors, are mediocre at best.

Bette Davis in *Dangerous*: not a classic.

That discussion hatched my first lecture illustrated with clips, "What Makes a Classic?" I used the *Dangerous* example, comparing that to *All About Eve*, a film that if anything has improved with age. Why do we remember Jimmy Stewart in *Mr. Smith Goes to Washington* and not in *Born to Dance*? Or Katharine Hepburn in *Bringing Up Baby* and not in *Break of Hearts*?

I presented twelve clips with the stories of how the films were made, and discussed the unique qualities that keep us going back for more viewings. The technology for showing clips from a laptop was still in the future (for me, anyway). I sent a pile of DVDs to Paul Gittelsohn's VIDEOSyncracies shop in South Burlington, with notes on which scenes to capture. Paul put them all on a single DVD disc that I projected at the library.

Although I had taught one film class at Goddard College in the 1980s and another at Community College of Vermont in the 1970s, I still did not think of myself as a public speaker. One of my least favorite parts of operating the Savoy was going in front of the audience to make an announcement, whether to introduce a speaker or to say "There will a short delay while we figure out what's wrong with the projector."

The "classics" program at the library was a turning point for me: I became at ease talking to an audience. It helped that I had knowledge to share and enthusiasm for my subject. I have subsequently repeated this program on several occasions throughout Vermont. It always sparks an animated discussion about the audience members' own favorites.

I have no trouble recalling the date of the initial library event— October 18, 2004—as it took place during the crucial fifth game of the Boston Red Sox and New York Yankees American League playoff series. Since New England is Red Sox country, I was not expecting a big crowd at the library, but to my surprise the room was full. Our librarian friend George Spaulding stuck his head in at occasional intervals to keep people apprised of the seesawing score.

•

In 2008, I was asked by Cindy McCloud, then director of the Montpelier Senior Activity Center, if I'd be interested in teaching a film course. My trial run was with a sure-fire genre: romantic comedies (*The Lady Eve* and *Roxanne* are two I remember showing). More people registered for the course than we had anticipated, and it was very enjoyable for me to share some of my favorites.

Preston Sturges' *The Lady Eve*, one of the great romantic comedies

That started a long relationship with MSAC, as it is known. I curated film series on, among other subjects, Comedies of the Depression, Family Relationships, Classics of the 1940s, and Documentaries. Whenever I described my MSAC teaching experience to friends in academia, they were envious: no assigned reading, no term papers, no grades, plus the added attraction that everyone who signs up wants to be there.

One problem, however, was that I was limited to English-language films due to sight line problems in the MSAC classroom. Many of us have had the challenging experience of watching a subtitled film in rooms with a level floor, whether a college classroom, institutional dining hall, or church basement. When the first subtitles appear, there is usually a flurry of seat-switching activity, followed by two hours of neck craning. Such was the case at the MSAC classroom.

The solution was just down the street, in familiar territory: in 2015, the class moved over to the Savoy, during the daytime when the theater was closed. With a sloped floor more amenable to subtitle-reading, I taught classes in the films of Chinese director Zhang Yimou, European films about immigration, films about post–World War II Europe, and many others. By my count, I've taught about 50 eight-week sessions for MSAC, with no end in sight.

The content was not all somber. At the end of the spring session of 2016, a regular attendee suggested a summer class called "Just for Fun." A great idea, I agreed. That was the first of three such summer series, with classics such as *Best in Show* and *Bringing Up Baby*, as well as my own lesser-known favorites, the British comedy *The Happiest Days of Your Life* (with Margaret Rutherford and Alastair Sim) and the brainy Marshall Brickman film *Simon* (with Alan Arkin as a professor who is brainwashed into believing he is a space alien).

•

I met Tony Keller in 2007 when he was planning an ambitious nine-hour extravaganza at Randolph's Chandler Music Hall to celebrate that historic building's centenary. After a long career as an arts administrator in Connecticut, Tony and his wife, the sculptor Karen Petersen, moved to the Randolph area in 2000, just a half-hour south of Montpelier. Tony and Karen quickly became involved in the vibrant arts scene of their adopted community. Among other activities, they helped raise $3.5 million for the expansion and renovation of the Chandler.

At the close of one showing at the 2011 Green Mountain Film Festival, Tony asked if I'd be interested in curating a series at the Chandler Music Hall. Tony was a longtime film buff, dating from his days as a Harvard undergraduate patronizing the Brattle Theater in Cambridge in the late 1950s. There was now a recently refurbished room upstairs from the main hall—named the Esther Mesh Room, in honor of a beloved Randolph music teacher—that was just the right size for a fifty-person audience.

This was the beginning of six years of films on Sunday nights, featuring a once-a-month film showing for eight months of the year. Sometimes there was a theme (comedies, literary adaptations) and sometimes a mix of genres and/or international films. There was often a potluck dinner before the films and an in-depth discussion afterward. The lively camaraderie of these film lovers, many of whom I would not have met in Montpelier, deepened my appreciation of this somewhat insular community.

A chance remark by my friend, cartoonist Ed Koren, led to another twist in my post-Savoy life. "I really enjoy your discussions," Ed offered, as I set up for one Randolph show, "but I'm afraid I'm kind of a film philistine." I responded with surprise that I had the impression he was a keen appreciator of many kinds of film. But what he meant by the term "philistine" was that he didn't know anything about what goes into the making of a film. "Perhaps you should think about offering a film-appreciation seminar?"

I broached the subject to Tony, who, thinking positively as always, set out to make it happen. For the next five winters, I taught film appreciation at a seminar, each consisting of three sessions. Here is a description of the "Looking Closely at Movies" seminar for that first winter, taken from my flyer:

Using the work of American, European and Asian directors as examples, I will present an inside view of the filmmaking process that will help sharpen our understanding of what is happening when we experience a film. We'll be watching many clips from Hollywood and foreign classics, studying the work of many directors. The first session will cover basic film vocabulary, film's Silent Era and the evolution of cinematic language. Session #2 will explore Hollywood's "Golden Age" and foreign film directors of the '30s and '40s. In Session #3, I'll look at four master foreign directors of the '50s and '60s (Kurosawa, Bergman, Fellini, and Truffaut) and how they influenced their American counterparts.

In subsequent years, the topics varied: editing, cinematography, and music; collaborations between actors and directors; films of the

1960s; independent films. By this time, I was able to capture DVD clips on my own Mac laptop, which made preparing these programs infinitely easier.

The seminar format was appealing for its intimacy. After the first successful three-session seminar in Randolph, I offered it closer to home as well, with sessions in Montpelier, Calais, and Marshfield.

•

You might say that I owe my twelve-years-and-counting association with the Vermont Humanities Council to Harper Lee. In 2011, the "Vermont Reads" selection of the Vermont Humanities Council was *To Kill a Mockingbird*. The idea for the "Vermont Reads" program had originated in Manchester, Vermont, in 2003, when the Mark Skinner Library and Northshire Bookstore planned a community-wide read; the book was *Witness* by Vermont author Karen Hess. The two organizations offered free books to the community and held different

To Kill a Mockingbird was my first film as a Vermont Humanities Council speaker.

events to encourage everyone to participate. The idea intrigued the Humanities Council, which took it statewide the following year.

In 2011, sixty Vermont towns participated in the program. Since both the central office of the Humanities Council and the Savoy Theater are in Montpelier, the organizers asked Terry Youk, the new owner of the Savoy, to host a screening of the 1962 film version of *To Kill a Mockingbird*, starring Gregory Peck as Atticus Finch. They also asked me if I could lead a discussion afterward.

I read all I could about the production of the film: how screenwriter Horton Foote was initially reluctant to write the screenplay because he revered the novel and was afraid of not doing it justice; how producer Alan J. Pakula and director Robert Mulligan recreated Harper Lee's hometown on a Hollywood sound stage; and how young Mary Badham got the coveted role of Scout Finch.

Just a year earlier I had been reading about Mary Badham in Diane McWhorter's memoir, *Carry Me Home*. McWhorter wrote of growing up white and privileged in Birmingham, Alabama. McWhorter was an elementary school classmate of Badham's and described her first viewing of the film, on a class trip: "We nodded appreciatively at Atticus Finch's words of wisdom and we recognized Calpurnia as a dead ringer for the fussy black women of our own kitchens. But soon our minds balked at the racial world of Scout's Alabama. For the first time, we came face-to-face with the central racial preoccupation of the southern white psyche, the dynamics that justified and ennobled Our Way of Life: the rape of a white woman by a black man. We had only a technical understanding of the crime, but neither did we know the meaning of southern justice."

McWhorter described crying at the fate of Jim Robinson and immediately having the thought, "If only my daddy could see me crying over the fate of a Black man." She says, "I still could not contain my tears. For the next few Sundays, my friends and I would go the matinees and weep clandestinely."

The passages in McWhorter's book gave me all the "hook" I needed to prepare the discussion, which continued for a half-hour after the film's end. I only dimly realized that the entire Montpelier staff of the

Humanities Council was in the first two rows. As the evening came to an end, Mark Fitzsimmons, who had organized the event for the Humanities Council, approached me and wondered if I knew about one of their programs, called the Vermont Speakers' Bureau. He explained that if I were listed in the Speakers' Bureau, a library or other nonprofit institution could invite me to present a program. The Humanities Council would pay my speaker's fee. It seems that in addition to a successful film showing that night, I unknowingly had had an audition for the Speakers' Bureau.

Since then, I've presented programs—on Alfred Hitchcock, films of the 1950s, the Hollywood blacklist, and others—to more than fifty Vermont libraries. I've been in places I never would have had any reason to visit, ranging from the ornate Bixby Library in Vergennes, complete with rotunda, to the tiny Ascutney Library, which could barely fit fifteen people plus my projector and screen. I've considered it an amazing gift to travel the state, meeting extraordinary people, both librarians and audience members.

Shortly after I started my Speakers' Bureau programs, I had what I called a post-Savoy epiphany. If on any night at the theater, there were twenty customers, my thought often was, "Where are the other fifty we need to break even?" But speaking at one library or another, my thought was instead, "Wow, twenty people—this is going to be good." It was just as our filmmaker friend Judith Helfand had told us: "I guess they are the right twenty people."

•

One day in 2007, Andrea and I took a walk around nearby Sodom Pond with our good friend Margaret Harmon. Margaret was excited about her involvement in a new program that was about to be launched in Vermont: the Osher Lifelong Learning Institute (OLLI).

A few years earlier, the Bernard Osher Foundation had started a network of classes for older students. The prospectus claimed that "the interest of many older adults, especially those who have retired, is in learning for the joy of learning—without examinations or grades— and keeping in touch with a larger world." By 2005, universities and colleges in all fifty states had set up courses in a wide variety of subjects.

In Vermont, the sponsoring institution for the Osher Foundation was the University of Vermont, which coordinated classes in nine Vermont towns, including Montpelier. Margaret was involved with the Montpelier branch from the start, and she asked if I wanted to teach a film class. The format she suggested was showing and discussing three films per semester, organized around a theme.

The first few semesters featured three films each by Alfred Hitchcock, Billy Wilder, and Preston Sturges. When I stop to count, I realize that I've presented twenty-eight different OLLI sessions, comprising eighty-four films. The structure of only three films per session has given me a lot of leeway in choosing themes, unlike, say, a twelve-week course.

The "learning for the joy of learning" aspect was certainly true. The students, all over sixty years old, were as engaged as any class could be. I found myself challenged to match them, coming up with themes that would stretch my own knowledge. Sometimes I studied as I might have for a final exam in college. For a three-film series on Czechoslovakia under communism (*The Firemen's Ball*, *Kolya*, and *Divided We Fall*), I read an astonishing memoir by Heda Margolius Kovály called *Under a Cruel Star*. Kovály and her husband Rudolf Margolius both survived death camps; Margolius joined the new communist government in 1948 and, as a Jew, was scapegoated in an infamous show trial and hanged in 1952. The agonizing history of twentieth century Czechoslovakia underlay the dark humor of those three films.

Over the years for OLLI, I studied up on the Irish "Troubles," the history of television, the remarkable life of Ruth Prawer Jhabvala (the writing partner of producer Ismail Merchant and director James Ivory),[46] the Iranian filmmaker Asghar Farhadi, and Graham Greene's screenwriting career.

There is no substitute for life experience in discussing some films. One semester featured the first three films of François Truffaut: *The*

---

[46]Prawer Jhabvala came from a German Jewish family who barely escaped to England in 1939. She became a British citizen in 1948, then moved to India upon marrying Cyrus Jhabvala, an architect. She published her first novel in 1955 and met Merchant and Ivory in 1963, when they wanted to film her novel *The Householder*. The Merchant-Ivory-Jhabvala team made twenty films together.

400 Blows, *Shoot the Piano Player*, and *Jules and Jim*. After watching the last film, starring Jeanne Moreau as the free-spirited but destructive femme fatale Catherine, a seventy-something woman raised her hand. "I haven't seen this movie since college, when I wanted to be as uninhibited as Catherine," she explained. "Now I think, Somebody please lock this woman up before she does any more harm!" A lively discussion followed about the perils of revisiting the films that made an emotional impact in our impressionable youth.

•

In 1993, a thoughtful gift from a friend turned out to have a ripple effect that has lasted until the present. John Irwin knew I was a movie buff and he had heard me talk about the Hollywood blacklist. He thought of me when he spotted *The Hollywood Writers' Wars* in a used bookstore.

The 1982 book relates how the formation of the Screen Writers Guild in the 1930s split the closely-knit movie community and led directly to the blacklist. The book grew out of a Columbia University Master's of Fine Arts thesis by Nancy Lynn Schwartz, who died suddenly at age twenty-six with the work almost completed. It was finished and published by her mother, Sheila Schwartz.

I thought I knew something about the history of the Hollywood Left, but this book was a revelation. The blacklist did not simply take shape as a result of anticommunist hysteria in post–World War II America; its roots went back to the formation of the Hollywood studio system, the anti-union sentiment of the Hollywood moguls, and the writers (many of them on the Left) who came in great numbers to Los Angeles after sound was introduced in 1927.

Nancy and Sheila Schwartz described the growth of the Communist Party among the screenwriters, and how the Nazi-Soviet Pact of 1939 sundered many friendships. It was unthinkable that the Soviets, after being the Nazis' chief adversaries since the rise of Hitler, could make such an about-face. But now support of the pact was an article of faith, and most American Communist Party members hewed to the new party line. Many others resigned their memberships rather than contort themselves into a position they didn't support. In a telling anecdote, the

The "Hollywood Ten" leave for prison.

Schwartzes quoted the memoir of a stalwart Communist Party member, screenwriter Donald Ogden Stewart. Stewart recalled his tears of joy and relief when the Nazis subsequently attacked the Soviet Union in June 1941; now everyone was on the same political side, and he could talk to his old friends again.

Once I began presenting programs for the Vermont Humanities Council, I thought of this slim but powerful book as an inspiration for a presentation on the history of the blacklist. I went back to read it again, this time taking detailed notes. The next step was finding film clips: the patriotic 1945 short *The House I Live In* was the first one that came to mind. The script was written by Albert Maltz. The idealistic title song, sung by Frank Sinatra, was written by Earl Robinson and Abel Meeropol (a.k.a. Lewis Allen). Ironically, the creators of this short film—Robinson, Meeropol, and Maltz—all became victims of the blacklist several years later due to their left-wing associations.

The rest fell into place quickly: *High Noon*, which Carl Foreman wrote as a blacklist parable; *Guilty by Suspicion*, with Robert DeNiro as a film director caught up in the Red Scare; the remarkable 1954 drama *Salt of the Earth*, written and directed by three blacklist victims; and

Zero Mostel, blacklisted in Hollywood.

The Front, with Woody Allen and Zero Mostel (himself a blacklist target).

I presented this program first at the 2014 Green Mountain Film Festival. Two years later, with the arrival of the Trump era, the material became even more timely.

•

At the time the Savoy opened with *Casablanca* in 1981, the concept of "virtual film classes" would have been in the realm of futuristic fiction. But soon after the start of the Covid-19 pandemic in 2020, I began using this platform to teach film history. At first, I was a grudging adaptor of this new technology, but I quickly grew to appreciate its potential; creating my Zoom seminars—initially a makeshift response to the pandemic—became an immensely gratifying experience. The classes I've taught since then have also provided a new appreciation of the role that film has played at each stage of my life.

I've done a session called "From a Child's Point of View," which included a clip from *The Bicycle Thieves,* a film I saw for the first time at summer camp when I was thirteen. I had never even heard of "Italian neorealism" at the time, but I was moved by the immediacy of this film, shot with nonprofessional actors on the streets of post–World War II Rome.

A class on Burt Lancaster featured two films I saw with my parents, *Birdman of Alcatraz* and *Seven Days in May,* plus two films—*Local Hero* and *Atlantic City*—that were early crowd-pleasers at the Savoy Theater.

The British thriller *Dead of Night* was a highlight of one session on "Ghosts and the Supernatural." I still get the shivers when I think of this film, one of many that I saw (instead of studying) during my senior year at the University of California, Berkeley. Four years later, after I had relocated to Vermont, it was the film I chose to inaugurate the first season of the Savoy's antecedent, the Lightning Ridge Film Society.

There were two lively Zoom conversations with film critics Peter Rainer and Gerald Peary, both past guests at Montpelier's Green Mountain Film Festival, and another with cinematographer Tom Hurwitz, one of my Columbia College classmates and a moviegoing pal in the mid-1960s.

A class on "Great French Actresses: 1930 to the Present" gave me the opportunity to introduce students to the luminous Arletty, star of *Children of Paradise*. That brought back memories on putting on those white gloves at the Carnavalet Museum in Paris while I was research-ing the film.

I'm planning future classes on Buster Keaton, Barbara Stanwyck and the thematically daring "pre-Code" Hollywood films of the 1930s, films set in the Irish countryside, and more. There are always old favorites to revisit and an always-growing list of films I want to see for the first time. There are fresh topics to explore, new national cinemas—whether South Korean, Romanian, Argentinian, and more—to discover.

The story that started in the very suburban county of Westchester, New York, and led to more than fifty years as a champion of film culture in Central Vermont is still unfolding. It's been a life of watching, showing, teaching, exploring—and loving—movies.

John O'Brien's Savoy-themed homage to the artist Saul Steinberg.

It Takes
A Crew

Acknowledgments

In the summer of 2021, three years after publishing my first book, *Red Scare in the Green Mountains,* I had been gathering research for a book on how Vermont's political activists organized against the Vietnam War. That project was losing steam, and I was feeling increasingly burdened by it. When I confessed as much to my wife, Andrea Serota, she suggested I write about something a lot closer to my heart—movies. By that evening, I had an outline of this book. Andrea's been an eager reader and collaborator through all my drafts and rewrites. It's been a special satisfaction to recollect together our years working at the Savoy Theater and the Green Mountain Film Festival.

I knew from the outset that Will Lindner would be the ideal editor for this project. I've known Will for years as a friend and fellow musician, but this book gave me a chance to witness his impressive talents as a wordsmith and shaper of sometimes unwieldy material.

Graphic designer Mason Singer has been a creative force in Central Vermont since the early 1970s, and we've happily worked together over the years. This book is proof that he remains a font (so to speak) of ingenious design ideas.

It's been a pleasure to work again with my old friend—going back to kindergarten—Laurie Lieb, copy editor supreme.

Thanks to the Rootstock Publishing team: especially Stephen McArthur and Samantha Kolber. Not every author is so fortunate to have an engaged publisher, always available—and just twenty minutes away. Long live independent publishers!

Ellen David-Friedman, Gary Ireland, Kathy Nemser, Ken Eisen, Charles Morrissey, John Morrison, and Laura Goldbaum read early drafts and contributed helpful suggestions and comments. A special thanks goes to Howard Norman, who read the manuscript at several stages and always steered me right.

Thanks to Stephen Bissette, Tony Klein, Tom Blachly, Norman Bloom, and Anne LaBrusciano for their memories of the Lightning Ridge Film Society, and to Susan Ritz, Chris Wood, Dianne Maccario, and Susan Sussman for their recollections of the Green Mountain Film Festival. Jim Higgins was eager to recount his memories of the "Flood of '92," and Jeffrey Jacobs shared insights about the film-distribution scene of the 1980s and 1990s. My brother Jon Winston refreshed my memory of the Savoy's construction. Susan Sussman also provided an archive of festival material.

Joe Yranski, Brian Beloverac, and Bruce Goldstein provided valuable guidance in tracking down photo permissions.

Some longtime friends of the Savoy Theater also made this book possible: Karen Jenney, Curtis and Ed Koren, Jane Pincus, Nat and Martha Winthrop, Mark Tannenbaum and Anne-Marie Gassier, Anne Sarcka, Chris and Ellen Lovell, Steve Worona, Karen and Richard Saudek, Matt Weinstein, Patricia Fontaine, Janet MacLeod, Barbara Weedon, Frank and Ducky Donath, Andrew London, Barbara McGrew, and Tony and Joan Beard.

Without the support of hundreds of central Vermont filmgoers, the Savoy would have closed its doors not long after we opened them, and there would be no book. Thank you all again for the difference you make in the cultural life of our community.

Endnotes

Chapter 1

Marjorie Heins's Priests of Our Democracy: The Supreme Court, Academic Freedom, and the Anti-Communist Purge (New York: New York University Press, 2013) taught me a great deal about the anxieties my parents must have faced during the Red Scare.

Although books about Alfred Hitchcock could fill a small library, the one I return to is François Truffaut's *Truffaut/Hitchcock* (New York: Simon and Schuster, 1983). The story of the two directors' relationship and how the book came into being is also the subject of Kent Jones's documentary of the same title.

Ronald Neame's entertaining memoir *Straight From the Horse's Mouth* (London: Scarecrow Press, 2003) recounts directing *The Horse's Mouth,* written by and starring Alec Guinness; Neame also wrote about his experiences working with David Lean, Michael Powell, and many luminaries of British film.

Chapter 2

In Peter Rainer's introduction to his collected reviews, *Rainer on Film* (Solana Beach, CA: Santa Monica Press, 2013), he recalls his early movie-watching days in ways that parallel my own.

I discovered Ellen Shrecker's scholarship when I was researching the years of the Red Scare. Two excellent books by her are *Many Are the Crimes* (Princeton: Princeton University Press, 1999), a comprehensive study of the time, and *No Ivory Tower* (New York: Oxford University Press, 1986), which focuses on McCarthyism and academia.

I was surprised to learn that Simon Callow is not only a brilliant actor, but a first-rate writer and film scholar as well. *The Road to Xanadu* (New York: Viking Press, 1996), the first book of his projected four-volume biography of Orson Welles, covers Welles's life through the release of *Citizen Kane*.

Chapter 4

The touchstone books I mention here are Parker Tyler's *Classics of the Foreign Film* (New York: Citadel Press, 1962, revised 1972) and Arthur Knight's *The Liveliest Art* (New York: Macmillan, 1957).

Toby and Dan Talbot operated the New Yorker Theater, as well as the distribution company New Yorker Films. Toby wrote an excellent account of those years in *The New Yorker Theater and Other Scenes From a Life at the Movies* (New York: Columbia University Press, 2009). She also edited her husband's posthumously published memoir, *In Love with Movies: From New Yorker Films to Lincoln Plaza Cinemas* (New York: Columbia University Press, 2022).

No one has captured the excitement of going to the movies in the early 1960s better than Phillip Lopate in his essay "Anticipation of *La Notte*: The 'Heroic' Age of Moviegoing." The essay is reprinted in his collection *Totally, Tenderly, Tragically* (New York: Anchor Press, 1998).

David Bordwell paid tribute to Parker Tyler, James Agee, and other film critics in his book *The Rhapsodes: How 1940s Critics Changed American*

Film Culture (Chicago: University of Chicago Press, 2016). Bordwell has written voluminously on film and, together with Kristin Thompson, writes one of the finest film blogs, *Observations on Film Art.*

Chapter 5

Andrew Sarris wrote about film with deep knowledge and lively enthusiasm. One of my favorites of his is *You Ain't Heard Nothin' Yet: The American Talking Film* (New York: Oxford University Press, 1998). The Kael-Sarris feud is covered in Brian Kellow's *Pauline Kael: A Life in the Dark* (New York: Viking Press, 2011) and in Molly Haskell's memoir *Love and Other Infectious Diseases* (New York: iUniverse, 2000).

Chapter 6

My Columbia College classmate Jerry Avorn wrote the definitive history of the tumult of 1968 in *Up Against the Ivy Wall* (New York: Atheneum Press, 1968). Paul Cronin recently revisited those events in his oral history *A Time to Stir: Columbia '68* (New York: Columbia University Press, 2020). The tumultuous spring of 1969 is detailed in Tom Dalzell's *The Battle for People's Park, Berkeley 1969* (Berkeley, CA: Heyday Press, 2019).

At odd moments, I love to dip into James Agee's brilliant film writing. He was the master of the "I loved it, but it could have been even better" review. Many reviews and essays he wrote for *The Nation* and *Time* are collected in *Agee on Film: Criticism and Comment on the Movies* (New York: Modern Library Press, 2000).

Patrick McGilligan has written insightful biographies of Nicholas Ray, George Cukor, Jack Nicholson, and many others. His book *Fritz Lang: The Nature of the Beast* (Minneapolis: University of Minnesota Press, 1998) punctured many of Lang's self-serving myths.

Chapter 7

Two exhaustive histories of Goddard College were published right down the road from me: Frank Adams and Ann Giles Benson's *To Know for Real: Royce S. Pitkin and Goddard College* (Adamant, VT: Adamant Press, 1987) and Forest Davis's *Things Were Different in Royce's Day: Royce S. Pitkin As Progressive Educator, a Perspective from Goddard College, 1950–1967* (Adamant, VT: Adamant Press, 1997).

Chapter 8

The book that led to the formation of the Lightning Ridge Film Society was *Stanley Kubrick Directs* by Alexander Walker (New York: Harcourt Brace and Jovanovich, 1972).

Stuart Klawans takes a line from the film *The Lady Eve* for the title of a biography, *Preston Sturges: Crooked But Never Common* (New York: Columbia University Press, 2023). Sturges's widow Sandy Sturges edited an invaluable work, *Preston Sturges by Preston Sturges: His Life in His Words* (New York: Touchstone Press, 1991).

Among the many film studies textbooks that Bruce Kawin has written is *How Movies Work* (New York: Macmillan, 1987, revised 1992); I found this book invaluable as I prepared to teach my own classes.

Two fascinating books on the emigrés who landed in Hollywood are John Russell Taylor's *Strangers in Paradise* (New York: Holt, Rinehart and Winston, 1983) and Donna Rifkind's *The Sun and Her Stars: Salka Viertel and Hitler's Exiles in the Golden Age of Hollywood* (New York: Other Press, 2020).

The late Yvonne Daley describes the enormous changes in Vermont around the time of my arrival in *Going Up the Country: When the Hippies, Dreamers, Freaks, and Radicals Moved to Vermont* (Hanover, NH: University Press of New England, 2018).

Chapter 9

Regarding the "Rastus" films, the subject of black representation in Hollywood films is a disturbing and fascinating one. Henry Louis Gates takes a broad view in *Stony the Road: Reconstruction, White Supremacy, and the Rise of Jim Crow* (New York: Penguin, 2020), while Donald Bogle focuses on films in *Toms, Coons, Mulattoes, Mammies, and Bucks: An Interpretive History of Blacks in American Films* (New York: Bloomsbury Academic, 2016, originally published 1973).

Casablanca was the Savoy's opening film in 1981 and was shown on several anniversaries over the years. The particular resonance of this film is explored in Aljean Harmetz's *Round Up the Usual Suspects: The Making of Casablanca—Bogart, Bergman, and World War II* (New York: Hyperion, 1993) and Noah Isenberg's *We'll Always Have Casablanca: The Life, Legend, and Afterlife of Hollywood's Most Beloved Movie* (New York: W.W. Norton, 2017).

Chapter 10

The National Society of Film Critics published several rich anthologies of critical essays. The one I quote in this chapter is from *Produced and Abandoned* (San Francisco: Mercury House, 1990). There were also volumes dedicated to non-American classics *(Foreign Affairs),* controversial films *(Love and Hisses),* and sex, violence, and censorship *(Flesh and Blood).*

Bridge of Light: Yiddish Film Between Two Worlds (New York: Museum of Modern Art, 1991) by longtime Village Voice film critic J. Hoberman is the definitive guide to this almost-forgotten slice of film history.

The behind-the-scenes work of John Pierson played a crucial role in the "indie revolution" of the 1980s. In his book *Spike, Mike, Slackers, and Dykes* (New York: Hyperion Press, 1995), he relates the inside story of how influential films like Spike Lee's *She's Gotta Have It* and Michael Moore's *Roger and Me* came to public attention.

Chapter 12

Kings of the Bs: Working within the Hollywood System, ed. Charles Flynn and Todd McCarthy (New York: E.P. Dutton, 1975) was one of the reference books in our Downstairs Video library. It was the place to learn about directors and producers such as Herschel Gordon Lewis, Edgar G. Ulmer, and Val Lewton.

Chapter 17

Molly Haskell brings a unique sensibility to her writings on the role of women on the screen. I enjoy her collection of essays, *Holding My Own in No Man's Land* (New York: Oxford University Press, 1977).

David Thomson's *The New Biographical Dictionary of Film* (New York: Alfred A. Knopf, 2014, revised, originally published 1975) is the one reference book to have handy when enjoying older films. He is erudite, witty, insightful, and fearless when it comes to challenging popular conceptions.

Kenneth Turan has written several film books; one I recommend is *Not to Be Missed: Fifty-four Favorites from a Lifetime of Film* (New York: Public Affairs Press, 2014).

Chapter 20

The New York Times obituary for Heda Kovály in 2010 sent me on a search for *Under a Cruel Star: A Life in Prague, 1941–1968* (New York: Holmes and Meier, 1997). It's an amazing story of one person's experience of several twentieth-century upheavals, and it colored my subsequent viewing of Eastern European films.

Ingmar Bergman's *The Magic Lantern: An Autobiography* reveals much about the sources of this great artist's creativity (Chicago: University of Chicago Press, 1997).

Diane McWhorter's *Carry Me Home: Birmingham, Alabama: The Climactic Battle of the Civil Rights Revolution* (New York: Simon and Shuster, 2013, originally published 2002) combines journalism with a deeply personal story.

My knowledge of the Hollywood blacklist was considerably augmented by *The Hollywood Writers' Wars,* by Nancy Lynn Schwartz (New York: McGraw Hill, 1982). I also recommend *Tender Comrades: A Backstory of the Hollywood Blacklist* (Minneapolis: University of Minnesota Press, 2012) by Patrick McGilligan and Paul Buhle.

Image Credits

Chapter 1

Stanley Kubrick's Taft High School photo; Leon Winston at Taft High School - author's collection

The Horse's Mouth - reprinted with permission of John Henderson

Chapter 3

Ilse and Ernst Bulova - courtesy of Buck's Rock Camp

Julia Winston at Buck's Rock - author's collection

David Holtzman's Diary - courtesy of Kino Lorber Films

Neighbours - reprinted with permission of the National Film Board of Canada

Chapter 4

The Cabinet of Dr. Caligari - courtesy of Kino Lorber Films

Children of Paradise - reprinted with permission of Pathé International Films

Chapter 5

William K. Everson - courtesy of William K. Everson Archive, New York University

Knife in the Water - reprinted with permission of John Henderson

Chapter 6

Columbia protest - photo by Richard Howard

Chapter 7

"The old Orr place" - courtesy of the Calais Historical Society

Walter Ungerer - courtesy of Goddard College Archives

Dennis Murphy - courtesy of Goddard College Archives

Chapter 8

Lightning Ridge Film Society program - author's collection

Chapter 9

News clippings - courtesy of the *Burlington Free Press* (photo by Dave Goska) and the *Times Argus*

Casablanca ads - courtesy of the *Times Argus*

FAQ card - author's collection

Rick Winston and Gary Ireland - courtesy of the *Times Argus*, photo by Betty Pirie

Savoy opening night - courtesy of the *Times Argus*, photo by Betty Pirie

Chapter 10

Movie ads - courtesy of the *Times Argus*

Savoy program - courtesy of Suzanne Rexford-Winston

Yiddish Culture Film Festival - author's collection

Chapter 11

David Wise - photo by Fred Wilber

Closing and reopening - courtesy of the *Times Argus*

Chapter 12

Video store photos and Downstairs Video catalog - author's collection

Tenth anniversary - courtesy of the *Times Argus*

Chapter 13

Ice jam - courtesy of the City of Montpelier

Flood photos - author's collection

Chapter 14

Jeffrey Jacobs – courtesy of Jeffrey Jacobs

Howards End – courtesy of the *Times Argus*

Chapter 15

Twenty-fifth anniversary – photo by Carlos Haase

Chapter 16

Chris Wood – courtesy of Jeb Wallace-Brodeur

A Healthy Baby Girl – courtesy of Judith Helfand, photo by Ted Helfand

La Ciudad – courtesy of David Riker

Montpelier demonstration – courtesy of the *Times Argus*, photo by Jeb Wallace-Brodeur

Film Festival cover – courtesy of Susan Sussman, photo by Emily Sloan

Chapter 17

Moving Midway – courtesy of Godfrey Cheshire

Molly Haskell – photo by Andrea Serota

Kenneth Turan and Rick Winston – photo by Patricia Williams

Chapter 18

Bob McQuillen – photo by Doug Plummer

Omnibus – courtesy of the heirs of Robert Saudek

Chapter 19

Burma VJ – author's collection

Fred Tuttle and John O'Brien – photo by Jack Rowell

Harvard Beats Yale 29-29 – courtesy of Kino Lorber Films

Chapter 20

Waiting in line – photo by Annie Tiberio

Audience in City Hall – courtesy of the *Times Argus*, photo by Stefan Hard

Chapter 21

Concession stand, office, and seat plaque – author's collection

Chapter 22

My Own Private Idaho, Next Stop Greenwich Village ads – courtesy of the *Times Argus*

Fahrenheit 911 line – courtesy of the *Times Argus*, photo by Tim Calabro

William Wegman poster– courtesy of the Film Society of Lincoln Center

Chapter 23

The Queen – courtesy of Paramount Pictures

Savoy for sale – courtesy of the *Burlington Free Press*

Juno ad – courtesy of the *Times Argus*

Chapter 24

The Seventh Seal – courtesy of Svensk Filmindustri

Chapter 25

Bill Morancy – photo by Erika Mitchell

Endnotes

Bookshelf – author's collection

About the Author

Rick Winston grew up in Yonkers, New York, and became hooked watching old films on TV at a young age. He went to Columbia College and University of California, Berkeley, where there were many opportunities to catch up on films while putting off writing English Literature papers.

Photo by Annie Tiberio

He moved to Vermont in 1970 and shortly afterward founded the Lightning Ridge Film Society, which morphed into the Savoy Theater in 1981. He was one of the founders of Montpelier's Green Mountain Film Festival and was its programming director until 2012. At the festival, he instituted a featured interview with a nationally-known film writer.

Rick and his wife Andrea Serota sold the Savoy in 2009. Since then, he has been teaching film at Burlington College, Community College of Vermont (Montpelier), and the Montpelier Senior Activity Center, while speaking on film subjects for the Vermont Humanities Council.

Some of his other interests and projects include historical research on Vermont during the McCarthy Era, and constructing twice-monthly "double crostic" puzzles for the *Times Argus/Rutland Herald*. His previous book, *Red Scare in the Green Mountains* (Rootstock, 2018) won the 2010 Richard O. Hathaway Award from the Vermont Historical Society for "Outstanding Contribution to Vermont History."

Visit his website: http://rickwinston.org.

More Nonfiction from Rootstock Publishing:

Alzheimer's Canyon: One Couple's Reflections on Living with Dementia by Jane Dwinell and Sky Yardley

The Atomic Bomb on My Back: A Life Story of Survival and Activism by Taniguchi Sumiteru

Catalysts for Change: How Nonprofits and a Foundation are Helping Shape Vermont's Future by Doug Wilhelm

China in Another Time: A Personal Story by Claire Malcolm Lintilhac

Collecting Courage: Anti-Black Racism in the Charitable Sector edited by Nneka Allen, Camila Vital Nunes Pereira & Nicole Salmon

Cracked: My Life After a Skull Fracture by Jim Barry

I Could Hardly Keep from Laughing: An Illustrated Collection of Vermont Humor by Don Hooper & Bill Mares

A Judge's Odyssey: From Vermont to Russia, Kazakhstan, and Georgia, Then on to War Crimes and Organ Trafficking in Kosovo by Dean B. Pineles

The Language of Liberty: A Citizen's Vocabulary by Edwin C. Hagenstein

A Lawyer's Life to Live: A Memoir by Kimberly B. Cheney

Nobody Hitchhikes Anymore by Ed Griffin-Nolan

Pauli Murray's Revolutionary Life by Simki Kuznick

Preaching Happiness: Creating a Just and Joyful World by Ginny Sassaman

Red Scare in the Green Mountains: Vermont in the McCarthy Era 1946-1960 by Rick Winston

Striding Rough Ice: Coaching College Hockey and Growing Up in the Game by Gary Wright

Tales of Bialystok: A Jewish Journey from Czarist Russia to America by Charles Zachariah Goldberg

Uncertain Fruit: A Memoir of Infertility, Loss, and Love by Rebecca and Sallyann Majoya

Walking Home: Trail Stories by Celia Ryker

You Have a Hammer: Building Grant Proposals for Social Change by Barbara Floersch

Also publishing fiction, poetry, and children's literature.
Visit our website www.rootstockpublishing.com to learn more.